Integrated English

TRANSITIONS

2

STUDENT BOOK

Linda Lee

Oxford University Press

Oxford University Press
198 Madison Avenue
New York, NY 10016 USA

Great Clarendon Street
Oxford OX2 6DP England

Oxford New York

Athens Auckland Bangkok Bogota
Buenos Aires Calcutta Cape Town Chennai Dar es Salaam
Delhi Florence Hong Kong Istanbul Karachi
Kuala Lumpur Madrid Melbourne
Mexico City Mumbai Nairobi Paris São Paulo Singapore
Taipei Tokyo Toronto Warsaw

and associated companies in
Berlin Ibadan

OXFORD is a trademark of Oxford University Press.

Copyright © 1999 Oxford University Press

Library of Congress Cataloging-in-Publication Data

Lee, Linda, 1950–
    Transitions 2: student book/Linda Lee.
    p. cm.—(Integrated English)
    ISBN 0-19-434630-7
    1. English language—Textbooks for foreign speakers. I
Title. II. Series.
    PE1128.L43 1999
428.2'4—dc21   98-33869

Senior Editor: Jeff Krum
Production Editor: Tyrone Prescod

Design Project Manager: Mark C. Kellogg
Design/Production Assistants: David Easter, Brett Sonnenschein
Senior Art Buyer: Alex Rockafellar
Art Buyer: Donna Goldberg
Picture Researcher: Clare Maxwell
Production Manager: Abram Hall
Production Controller: Georgiann Baran

Cover direction: Shelley Himmelstein
Cover design/photo montage: R. S. Winter

Printing (last digit): 10 9 8 7 6 5 4 3 2 1
Printed in Hong Kong

Illustrations by: Kathryn Adams/THREE IN A BOX INC.,
Steven Adler, Eliot Bergman, Mike Hertz Associates, Claudia C.
Kehrhahn, Scott MacNeill/MACNEILL & MACINTOSH, Cliff
Miller, Karen Minot, Olivia, Rodica Prato, Dean Rohrer, Rob
Schuster, Nina Wallace

Location and studio photography by: John Bessler, Dennis
Kitchen, Maggy Milner, Stephen Ogilvy, Ken Tannenbaum

**The publishers would like to thank the following for their
permission to reproduce photographs:** James L. Amos/Corbis;
AP/Wide World Photos; Art Resource; David Ball/The Stock
Market; Biondo Productions/Liaison International; John
Blaustein/Tony Stone Images; S. Brimberg/N. Aujolat/National
Geographic; Brown Brothers; David Burnett/Contact Press
Images; Buss/FPG; Bruce Byers/FPG; Camerique/H. Armstrong
Roberts; Charles Pelton Publications; Chris Cole/Duomo;
Comstock; Corbis/Bettmann; David Corio/Michael Ochs Archive,
Venice, Calif.; Marco Cristofari/The Stock Market; Culver
Pictures; Jim Cummins/FPG; Bob Daemmrich/Stock Boston;
Viren Desai/The Image Works; De Sazo/Photo Researchers;
Anthony Edgeworth/The Stock Market; Shaun Egan/Tony Stone
Images; Folio; Robert Frerck/The Stock Market; Robert
Frerck/Woodfin Camp; Robert Fried/DDB Stock Photo; Rob
Gage/FPG; Eduardo Gil/Black Star; Godlewski/Liaison
International; Samuel Goldwyn Co./The Everett Collection;
Steven Gottlieb/FPG; Steve Grubman/The Image Bank; Louise
Gubb/The Image Works; Christine Hanscomb/Tony Stone
Images; Thomas Hoepker/Magnum Photos; B. W.
Hoffmann/Envision; Ted Horowitz/The Stock Market; Chris
Jones/The Stock Market; Jump Run Productions/The Image
Bank; Wolfgang Kaehler/Liaison International; Yousef
Karsh/Woodfin Camp; Hilarie Kavanagh/Tony Stone Images;
Michael Keller/FPG; T. Kelly/Woodfin Camp; Calvin
Larsen/Photo Researchers; David Lassman/The Image Works;
John Lei/Stock Boston; Leonard Lessin/Peter Arnold; Thomas
Lindley/FPG; Dick Luria/FPG; J.B. Marshall/Envision; Mayo/The
Image Bank; Loren McIntyre/Woodfin Camp; H.P. Merten/The
Stock Market; John Mitchell/D. Donne Bryant; R. A.
Mittermeier/Bruce Coleman; Mugshots/The Stock Market; Lance
Nelson/The Stock Market; Fergus O'Brien/FPG; D. Ogust/The
Image Works; Masato Oishi/Shinkenchiku-Sha; Josef
Polleross/The Stock Market; Hans Reinhard/Bruce Coleman;
Rembrandt van Rijn/Rijksmuseum Foundation, Amsterdam;
Frances M. Roberts; Marc Romanelli/The Image Bank; Albert I.
Rose/Archive Photos; Luis Rosendo/FPG; Don Saban/Liaison
International; Chuck Savage/The Stock Market; Bob
Schatz/Liaison International; Mark Scott/FPG; Simpson/FPG;
Ariel Skelley/The Stock Market; Robin Smith/Tony Stone Images;
Tony Stone Images; Superstock; Tabuteau/The Image Works; H.
Takahashi Photography; Telegraph Colour Library/FPG; Laquita
Thompson/The Alabama Museum of Natural History, University
of Alabama; Topham/The Image Works; John Terence
Turner/FPG; Turner & Devries/The Image Bank; Mireille
Vautier/Woodfin Camp; Stephen Wade/Allsport; T.
Walker/Jacana/Photo Researchers; Warner Bros./Kobal
Collection; David Weintraub/Stock Boston; Fitzgerald Wilson
Turner/Liaison International; Kent Wood/Peter Arnold; Adam
Woolfitt/Corbis; Adam Woolfitt/Woodfin Camp; Mike
Yamashita/Woodfin Camp

**The publishers would also like to thank the following for their
help:** Acoustiguide Worldwide, Inc.; The Alabama Museum of
Natural History/University of Alabama; Carcool/Thousand Oaks
News Chronicle; Harley Davidson; Ryuko Iikubo of Look Japan,
Ltd.; The Japan Big Tree Society; Edd Lee/The Belleville News
Democrat; Marin Mountain Bikes; Suffolk University; Twentieth
Century Fox/Paramount Pictures; United Artists; Allen Ripp for
Tim & Nina Zagat

p. 1 Excerpted from Gregory Stock, Ph.D's THE BOOK OF
QUESTIONS. Illustration by Tom Lulevitch. Copyright © 1985,
1987 by Gregory Stock. Used by permission of Workman
Publishing Co., Inc., N.Y. All rights reserved.
p. 11 Excerpted from FACES' May 1994 issue: Hair, © 1994,
Cobblestone Publishing Company, 30 Grove Street, Suite C,
Peterborough, N.H. Reprinted by permission of the publisher.
p. 17 By Shel Silverstein. Copyright © 1974 by EVIL EYE
MUSIC, INC. Used by permission of HarperCollins Publishers.
p. 31 Adapted from an article in *Look Japan*. © December 1994.
Used with permission.
p. 37 Interview by Zack Hanle.
    BON APPÉTIT is a registered trademark of Advance
Magazine Publications, Inc. Copyright © 1998 by The Condé
Nast Publications, Inc. Reprinted with permission.
p. 45 Reprinted with the permission of Simon & Schuster Books
for Young Readers, an imprint of Simon & Schuster Children's
Publishing Division. Excerpted from THE MACMILLAN BOOK
OF FASCINATING FACTS: AN ALMANAC FOR CHILDREN by
Ann Elwood and Carol Orsag Madigan. Copyright © 1989 Ann
Elwood and Carol Orsag Madigan.
p. 65 *You've Got a Friend*. Words and music by Carole King. ©
1971 COLGEMS-EMI MUSIC, INC. All rights reserved.
International copyright secured. Used by permission.
p. 67 CALVIN AND HOBBES © 1993 Watterson. Dist. by
UNIVERSAL PRESS SYNDICATE. Reprinted with permission.
All rights reserved.
pp. 79–80 Text and art from *In My Family* © 1996 by Carmen
Lomas Garza. Reprinted with permission of the publisher,
Children's Book Press, San Francisco, Calif.

ACKNOWLEDGMENTS

The author and publisher would like to thank the following people for reviewing *Transitions*. Their comments and suggestions contributed to its development and helped shape its content.

Miguel Ivan Abreu, Instituto Tecnológico de Veracruz, Veracruz, Mexico

Ana Alaminos, Esc. Nal. Preparatoria No. 5-UNAM, Mexico City, Mexico

Timothy Allan, St. Mary's College, Nagoya, Japan

Daniel Altamirano, CENLEX-IPN, Mexico City, Mexico

Charles Anderson, Athénée Français, Tokyo, Japan

Lucia de Aragão, União Cultural, São Paulo, Brazil

Kevin Bandy, Boston English Learners, Caracas, Venezuela

Barbara Bangle, CELE-UAEM, Toluca, Mexico

Eleanor Kirby Barnes, Athénée Français, Tokyo, Japan

Erin Burke, Aichi Shukutoku Junior College, Nagoya, Japan

Diane Burnett, Tokyo Women's Christian University, Tokyo, Japan

Paul Cameron, International Trade Institute, Hsinchu, Taiwan

Kyung-Whan Cha, Chung Ang University, Seoul, Korea

Katie Chiba, Trident School of Languages, Nagoya, Japan

Steve Cornwell, Osaka Jogakuin Junior College, Osaka, Japan

Lynn Napoli Costa, ICBEU, Belo Horizonte, Brazil

Katy Cox, Casa Thomas Jefferson, Brasília, Brazil

Marion DeLarche, Kanda University of International Studies, Chiba, Japan

Jacob de Ruiter, CELE-UAEM, Toluca, Mexico

Montserrat Muntaner Djmal, IBEU, Rio de Janeiro, Brazil

Jasna Dubravcic, Showa Women's University, Tokyo, Japan

Ron Dziwenka, Yonsei University, Seoul, Korea

Elin Emilsson, Universidad National Autónoma de Mexico (UNAM), Mexico City, Mexico

Rosa Erlichman, Unãio Cultural, São Paulo, Brazil

Alejandra Gallegos, Interlingua, Aguascalientes, Ags., Mexico

Ismael Garrido, CELE-Benemérita Universidad Autónoma de Puebla, Puebla, Mexico

Peter Gobel, Ritsumeikan University, Kyoto, Japan

Noni Goertzen, Aichi Shukutoku Junior College, Nagoya, Japan

Ann-Marie Hadzima, National Taiwan University, Taipei, Taiwan

Pamela Hu, Taiwan Boys High School, Tainan, Taiwan

Diana Jones, Grupo Educativo Angloamericano, S.C., Mexico City, Mexico

Atsuko Kashiwagi, Showa Women's University, Tokyo, Japan

Koomi Kim, University of Arizona, Tucson, Ariz., USA

Mia Kim, Kyung-Hee University, Seoul, Korea

Jill Kinkaid, Seven Language School, São Paulo, Brazil

Hyun-Jung Kwon, Kyungil University, Taegu, Korea

Nick Lambert, Toyo University, Tokyo, Japan

Jean-Pierre Louvrier, IBEU-CE, Fortaleza, Brazil

Angus Macindoe, Aichi University, Miyoshi, Japan

Gabriela Martínez, CEMARC, Mexico City, Mexico

Bruce McAlpine, University of Toronto, Toronto, Canada

Katherine McDevitt, Universidad Autónoma Chapingo, Chapingo, Mexico

Anne Newell McDonald, Hajiyama University, Hiroshima, Japan

Jane McElroy, Aoyama Gakuin University, Tokyo, Japan

Anne McKnight, Yonsei University, Seoul, Korea

Elías Mennhar, Vizcainas School, Mexico City, Mexico

Joaquín Meza, Esc. Nal. Preparatoria No. 7-UNAM, Mexico City, Mexico

Joann Miller, Universidad del Valle, Mexico City, Mexico

Rick Nelson, Matsuyama University, Evergreen Language School, Matsuyama, Japan

Mary Sisk Noguchi, Meijo University Junior College, Nagoya, Japan

Terry O'Brien, Otani Women's University, Osaka, Japan

Sonia Ocampo, Bertha von Glumer School, Mexico City, Mexico

Gary Ockey, Kanda University of International Studies, Chiba, Japan

Mary Oliveira, IBEU, Rio de Janeiro, Brazil

Aída Orozco, Esc. Nal. Preparatoria No. 5-UNAM, Mexico City, Mexico

Dawn Paullin, Asia University, Tokyo, Japan

John Perkins, Tokyo Foreign Language College, Tokyo, Japan

Lara Perry, Time-Life English Language School, Yonago, Japan

Augustine Paul Porter, Grupo Educativo Angloamericano S.C., Mexico City, Mexico

César Regnier, CELE-Benemérita Universidad Autónoma de Puebla, Puebla, Mexico

Yolanda Reyes, Esc. Nal. Preparatoria No. 6-UNAM, Mexico City, Mexico

Carol Rinnert, Hiroshima City University, Hiroshima, Japan

Peggy Rule, St. Mary's College, Nagoya, Japan

Marie Adele Ryan, Associacão Alumni, São Paulo, Brazil

Jennifer Sakano, Keio Shonan Fujisawa High School, Fujisawa, Japan

Silvia Sandoval, Instituto Mexicano del Petroleo, Mexico City, Mexico

Debora Schisler, Seven Language School, São Paulo, Brazil

Tamara Swenson, Osaka Jogakuin Junior College, Osaka, Japan

Diane Urairat, Rangsit University, Patumtani, Thailand

Oscar Vásquez, Universidad del Valle, Mexico City, Mexico

Catherine Vellinga, University of Toronto, Toronto, Canada

Patricia Verduzco, CELEX-IPN, Mexico City, Mexico

M. Angel Vidagna, CECYT, Mexico City, Mexico

Roberto Viera, CAFAM, Bogotá, Colombia

Adele Villela, Universidad Latinoamericana, Mexico City, Mexico

Fu-Hsang Wang, Nan Tai College, Tainan, Taiwan

Julian Woolhouse, Japan College of Foreign Languages, Tokyo

Derek Wotton, UNAM, ENEP Iztacala, Mexico City, Mexico

The author and publisher would like to thank the following people for contributing ideas, personal stories, and cultural information for use in *Transitions 2*: Nick Alkemade and family, Claudio Amaral, Simon Byrne, Gemma Dickmann, Irene Frankel, Carmen Lomas Garza, Tadao Hiraoka, Victoria Kimbrough, Ellen Kisslinger, Yoko Tezuka, and Steve Ziolkowski.

The author would also like to the following people at OUP who offered many helpful insights and suggestions: Karen Brock, Julia Chang, Judith Cunningham, Bev Curran, Maria Amélia Dalsenter, Silvia Dones de Sauza, Chris Foley, Roy Gilbert, Robert Habbick, Todashi Kambara, Jung Ja Lee, Toshiki Matsuda, Paul Riley, and Andrew Todd.

Scope and Sequence

Listening	Reading	Process Writing (Workbook)
• Identifying questions • Listening for people's ideas and suggestions	• "Questions at an Art Museum" • "Empanadas" and "Blessing on the Wedding Day" (jigsaw reading) • "Fact Files" (Workbook)	Writing a fact file • Identifying your audience
• Listening for specific information about symbols	• "Dreadlocks" (an interview) • "Dreadlocks: A Summary" (Workbook)	Summarizing an interview • Summarizing • Using your own words
• Listening for information to confirm your predictions • Listening for details about people's opinions on gender roles	• "Facts About Men and Women" • "My Rules" (poem) • "Who Has It Better—Men or Women?" (Workbook)	Giving reasons • Collecting ideas
• Listening for details to complete a conversation • Listening for details to confirm a prediction	• "Hit by Lightning" • "The Burning Airplane" and "The Big Bang" (jigsaw reading) • "A Few Broken Ribs" (Workbook)	Telling a story • Quickwriting • Making a story map
• Listening to people tell about their pastimes. • Identifying specific questions	• "1,600 Giant Trees" • "Job Resumes" (Workbook)	Writing a resume • Collecting ideas • Organizing your ideas
• Listening to people describe different kinds of foods • Listening to people recommend restaurants	• "Food Facts" • "Tim and Nina Zagat" (an interview) • "The Black Cat" (Workbook)	Writing a review • Analyzing paragraphs
• Listening for information to confirm your predictions	• "The Origin of Everyday Things" • "A Cheap and Simple Solution" • "I Love Duct Tape" (Workbook)	Expressing an opinion • Giving examples • Listing ideas
• Listening for details about mysterious objects	• "Mysterious Things" • "The Mysterious Box" (folktale) • "Is There a Loch Ness Monster?" (Workbook)	Writing to inform • Making a cluster diagram • Using your own words
• Listening for people's opinions about rules and laws • Listening to someone describe the rules in his family	• "International Laws" • "Mom Goes on Strike" • "Should Students Be Allowed to Have Part-Time Jobs?" (Workbook)	Weighing the pros and cons • Getting your reader's attention
• Listening for what people would do in different situations • Listening to people tell what they would do for their friends	• "The Stingiest Man in the World" • "You've Got a Friend" (song) • "My Friend, Albert Einstein" (Workbook)	Describing a person • Using anecdotes
• Listening for the reasons behind people's wishes • Listening to and comparing different versions of a story	• A Calvin and Hobbes cartoon • "The Three Wishes" (play) • "The Owl and the Rabbits" (Workbook)	Writing a fable • Using dialogue • Making a story map
• Listening to people describe their feelings • Listening for the rest of a story	• "Memorable Moments" • "The Big Crash" (Workbook)	Describing a memorable moment • Quickwriting • Connecting ideas

Introduction

Integrated English

Integrated English is a four-skills program for adult and young adult students of American English. Comprised of three, two-book courses—*Gateways, Transitions,* and *Explorations*—this program takes students from beginner through intermediate levels. Recognizing that students' language learning needs change as they progress from one level to the next, the *Integrated English* program varies its approach to meet students' specific needs at each level.

Transitions

Transitions, the second course in the *Integrated English* program, is for students at a low-intermediate level. It features an innovative topic-based syllabus in which authentic content provides both a context for meaningful language work and a basis for the exploration of interesting adult topics.

Key Features of Transitions

- **Rich content** (photo collages, interviews, first-person accounts, captioned photos, charts and graphs, etc.) that provides students with reasons to confer, ask meaningful questions, seek clarification, share opinions, make comparisons, and agree or disagree.

- **Separate fluency-based and form-based activities.** Separating these activity types makes it clear to students when they can focus on communicating their ideas and when they should be focusing on a specific language structure.

- Fluency-based activities that provide students with **multiple opportunities to recycle** previously studied language structures and vocabulary. In essence, each unit in *Transitions* functions as a review unit of previously studied material.

- **A discovery approach to grammar** that gives students the opportunity to talk explicitly about language, and to ask questions and make and test hypotheses about a particular structure.

- **Task-based activities that integrate the skills of reading, writing, speaking, and listening.** For example, an activity in *Transitions* might ask pairs of students to come up with questions about a photograph, listen for answers to their questions and take notes, read to get more information, and then to relate what they learned to their own lives by completing a chart.

Components of Transitions

- **Student Book.** Each of the 12 units in *Transitions 2* is six pages long. A Strategy Session follows the third, sixth, and ninth units and introduces important conversation management strategies. The Grammar Guide in the back of the book can be used for in-class reference or at-home study.

- **Cassettes and CDs.** All listening activities, pronunciation exercises, conversations, and reading exercises in the Student Book are recorded. This symbol 📼 next to an exercise indicates that it is recorded.

- **Workbook.** The Workbook provides activities and exercises to supplement the material presented in the Student Book. This material can be used in class or done as homework. In addition, the Workbook provides a comprehensive process writing program.

- **Teacher's Book.** The Teacher's Book contains step-by-step suggestions for setting up and carrying out the activities in the Student Book. Background and cultural information related to the topic of the unit as well as Teaching Tips and Expansion Activities give teachers practical suggestions and ideas on how to adapt the material to their own teaching needs.

How Does a Unit in Transitions Work?

Each unit in *Transitions* is organized into two, three-page sections.
These three-page sections work as follows:

Presentation, Practice, and Interaction

1st page. The first page of each unit is the Presentation section. The activities in this section introduce the topic of the unit and get students to communicate their ideas using language they have studied previously.

2nd page. On the second page of each unit, the Practice section asks students to focus on a linguistic feature that came up naturally during the presentation of the unit topic. The activities on this page get students to investigate a particular grammatical structure and to experiment with using it.
  Cross-referenced to the Practice page, the Grammar Guide in the back of the book provides additional examples of the target structures, helpful tips on form and usage, plus a form-based exercise for extra grammar practice.

3rd page. The activities on the third page of each unit bring the students back to the unit topic and provide them with opportunities for genuine interaction. These activities give students a chance to "try out" the language structure from the previous page in a meaningful communicative context.

Preview, Exploration, and Expansion

4th page. The second half of the unit begins on the fourth page with the Preview section. The communicative activities on this page get students thinking and talking about a new aspect of the topic while also preparing them for a short reading on the following page.

5th page. A short reading on the fifth page gives students the opportunity to experiment with useful strategies such as reading for specific information and using context to guess the meaning of words. At the same time, the reading provides students with interesting ideas and information that they can react to and talk about.

6th page. The communicative activities on the sixth page of each unit get students to expand on the information in the reading and to apply this information to their own lives. These activities can also serve as a jumping-off point for additional project work and writing activities.

Before you start...

USEFUL EXPRESSIONS: *Asking for clarification*

1. *Pairs.* Use the expressions in the box to complete the conversations below.

How do you spell that?	What does *courageous* mean?
What's this called in English?	Could you repeat that?
How do you pronounce this word?	

a. **A** *How do you pronounce this word?*
   B Which one? This one?
   A Uh-huh. That one.
   B Treasured.
   A I'm sorry. _____?
   B Sure. Treasured.

b. **A** _____?
   B It means brave.

c. **A** How do you say ✈ in English?
   B Airplane.
   A _____?
   B Airplane? A-I-R-P-L-A-N-E.

d. **A** _____?
   B This?
   A Yeah. The place where the pilot sits.
   B It's called the cockpit.

2. Listen and check your answers.

USEFUL EXPRESSIONS: *Showing interest*

1. You can use the expressions below to show interest in what another person is saying. Listen to the conversations and write the missing expressions.

Uh-huh ...	Interesting ...	Really?
Hmmm ...	I see ...	Oh, yeah?

a. **A** Have you ever been on a boat?
   B Yes, I have.
   A *Really?* When?
   B Last year on vacation.
   A _____. And how was it?
   B It was really fun!

b. **A** I'd like to be famous someday.
   B _____. In what way?
   A I want to start my own rock band.
   B _____. Do you play an instrument?
   A Yes. I play the guitar and the piano.
   B _____. Guitar and piano! That's pretty good!
   A Thanks.

2. *Pairs.* Practice the conversations with your partner.

Topic: Questions
Language: Getting information
Focus: Question forms

PRESENTATION

1. We asked one person the questions below.
Match the questions with his answers.

The six questions on the left are from *The Book of Questions.*

Questions

a. Would you like to be famous? In what way?
b. What is your most treasured memory?
c. When did you last cry?
d. Who do you admire most? Why?
e. What do you dream of doing? Why haven't you done it yet?
f. What do you like about your life?

Answers

"Nelson Mandela. I think he's very courageous."

"My family. They're really great."

"I've always wanted to learn how to fly a plane, but I can't afford to take lessons."

"The time we went to Rio for Carnival."

"At the movies."

"Sure. I'd love to be a famous scientist."

2. *Pairs.* Take turns asking and answering the questions.

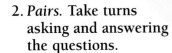

PRACTICE

1. *Pairs.* Read questions *a–e* below. Then answer the questions at the bottom of the box.

> **GETTING INFORMATION:** *Question forms*
> a. Would you like to be famous?
> b. When did you last cry?
> c. Who do you admire most?
> d. What do you like about your life?
> e. Have you ever told a lie?
>
> • Which questions ask about something that happened in the past?
> • Which questions ask you to answer *yes* or *no*?
> **Answers on page 93**

2. *Pairs.* Write new questions by changing the <u>underlined</u> words in the questions below.

   a. Would you like to be <u>famous</u>?
     Would you like to be <u>a teacher</u>?
     Would you like to be _____
     Would you like to be _____

   b. When did you last <u>cry</u>?
     When did you last <u>buy a gift for someone</u>?
     When did you last _____
     When did you last _____

   c. Who do you <u>admire most</u>?
     Who do you <u>talk to most</u>?
     Who do you _____
     Who do you _____

   d. What do you like about <u>your life</u>?
     What do you like about <u>your school</u>?
     What do you like about _____
     What do you like about _____

   e. Have you ever <u>told a lie</u>?
     Have you ever <u>ridden a motorcycle</u>?
     Have you ever _____
     Have you ever _____

Compare questions with your classmates.

3. Move around the class asking and answering questions from Activity 2.

🔊 PRONUNCIATION POINT: *Reduced forms*
/wʊdʒə/   /dɪdʒə/
Would you like to be ...?   When did you last ...?
Go to page 90.

LISTENING

1. Listen and check (✓) the questions you hear.

a. ☐ Where did you go last night?
☑ What did you do last night?

b. ☐ When did you go to sleep last night?
☐ When do you go to sleep at night?

c. ☐ Have you ever tried Indian food?
☐ Have you ever tried Italian food?

d. ☐ Who is your teacher?
☐ How is your teacher?

e. ☐ What's your favorite movie?
☐ Who's your favorite movie star?

f. ☐ Where do you buy your shoes?
☐ Where did you buy your shoes?

2. *Pairs.* Take turns asking and answering the questions.

WHAT'S THE QUESTION?

1. *Pairs.* Complete these questions with your own ideas.
Then share your questions with the class.

Ⓐ Where _____?
Ⓑ In New York.

Ⓐ Who _____?
Ⓑ Michael Jordan.

Ⓐ What _____?
Ⓑ *Titanic.*

Ⓐ When _____?
Ⓑ In December.

Ⓐ How many _____?
Ⓑ Ten.

Ⓐ What color _____?
Ⓑ Red.

2. *Pairs.* Write a question for each "answer" in the box
below. Then read your questions to the class and see
if your classmates can give you the correct answers.

ANSWERS	
English	New York
In January	Five
Australia	Blue
Elton John	The President of
Green	the United States
Last year	A computer
A hospital	Twelve

Example:

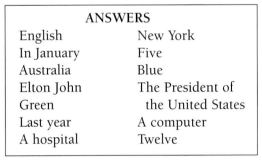

What language do they speak in Australia?

English.

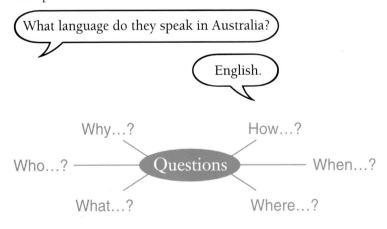

Why...?   How...?

Who...? —— Questions —— When...?

What...?   Where...?

PREVIEW

1. *Pairs.* Work together to answer these questions.

    a. Read the title of the article on page 5. What do you think the article is about?

    b. The painting on page 5 is in the Rijksmuseum in Amsterdam. What questions come to mind when you look at it?

2. We asked some people the questions below. Listen and complete their answers.

    a. Imagine that you work at the Rijksmuseum in Amsterdam. How could you get visitors to look carefully at the painting on page 5?

    Idea 1: Put magnifying glasses *next to all the paintings.*
    Idea 2: Give people _____.
    Idea 3: Have tour guides _____.
    _____
    _____

    b. How could you get more people to come to the Rijksmuseum to see its paintings?

    Idea 1: Give people *free coffee and sandwiches.*
    Idea 2: Open a _____.
    Idea 3: Make the museum _____ one night a week.
    _____
    _____

3. *Groups.* Work together to add two ideas of your own to each question. Then share your ideas with the class.

READ AND RESPOND

1. Read the article on page 5 and look for answers to the questions in the chart below.

Questions	Answers
a. What kinds of questions did visitors ask about Rembrandt's painting?	
b. What did the museum curators do with the visitors' questions?	
c. What was the result of this experiment?	

2. Compare answers with your classmates.

Questions at an Art Museum 📼

A few years ago, the curators* at the Rijksmuseum in Amsterdam conducted an interesting experiment. First, they collected all of the questions that visitors asked about the painting, "The Nightwatch" by Rembrandt.

"The Nightwatch" by Rembrandt

The visitors asked many different kinds of questions. Some people asked for general information about the painting:

How much does the painting cost?
Are there mistakes in the painting?

Some people asked about the content of the painting:

Who are the people in the picture?
Where are these people?

And some people asked questions about the painter:

When did Rembrandt paint this picture?
Why did he paint this picture?

The curators wrote answers to the visitors' questions. Then they put the questions and answers on the walls near the painting.

What was the result? Visitors spent much more time looking at the painting. Previously, visitors spent about six minutes looking at Rembrandt's painting. With the questions and answers, visitors spent about 30 minutes looking at it. They walked back and forth between the painting and the questions and answers. Visitors said the questions encouraged them to look at the painting more carefully and to remember more. According to the visitors, the questions helped them to see the painting in new ways.

---

*curators: directors of an art museum

ASK AND ANSWER

1. *Groups of four.* Divide your group into two teams:
   Team A and Team B. Then follow the instructions below.

   Team A: Write five questions about this painting.

Example:
Where are these people?
What are they doing?

Empanadas by Carmen Lomas Garza

   Team B: Write five questions about this painting.

Example:
Who is the man?
What is the woman in the white dress doing?

Blessing on the Wedding Day by Carmen Lomas Garza

2. Exchange questions with the other team. Then turn to the back
   of the book to answer the <u>other team's</u> questions.

   Team A: Go to page 79.
   Team B: Go to page 80.

Topic: **Symbols**
Language: **Getting information**
Focus: **Direct and indirect questions**

PRESENTATION

1. Look at the photographs. Do you know what these things are? Do you know what they symbolize?

2. Choose a word or phrase to complete each sentence below.

> eternal love and commitment
> democracy, peace, progress, justice, and equality
> the fight against AIDS
> the five major regions of the world
> good luck
> peace

a. The Olympic rings represent _____.

b. In some countries, a four-leaf clover is a symbol of _____.

c. The five stars on the flag of Singapore stand for _____.

d. The red ribbon has become a worldwide symbol of _____.

e. The wedding ring is a symbol of _____.

f. The two olive branches on the United Nations flag symbolize _____.

3. **Listen and check your answers.**

PRACTICE

1. Read questions *a–f* below. Then answer the
questions at the bottom of the box.

- Compare the direct and indirect questions above. What is different about the form of the questions?
- Which questions above can be answered with a *yes* or *no*?
- Look at question *f*. When do we use *if* in an indirect question?

Answers on page 94

2. We asked a Canadian the questions below.

a. What does the Canadian flag look like?
b. What is the national symbol of Canada?
c. When did British Columbia become a
Canadian province?
d. Who is the prime minister of Canada?
e. Is Canada a democracy?

**How would you ask your classmates the same
questions?**

a. Do you know *what the Canadian flag looks like?*
b. Do you know _____?
c. _____?
d. _____?
e. _____?

3. *Pairs.* Complete these conversations with direct
or indirect questions.

Ⓐ *Do you know where this money is from?*
　(where/this money/from)
Ⓑ Yes. It's from Korea.
Ⓐ _____?
　(whose picture/on it)
Ⓑ Of course. That's King Sejong.
Ⓐ I see. _____?
　(when/king)
Ⓑ In the 15th century. He was very famous.
Ⓐ Really? _____.
　(Why/famous)
Ⓑ He invented the Korean alphabet.
Ⓐ The king invented the alphabet! That's amazing!

🔊 **Listen and check your ideas.**

PRONUNCIATION POINT: *Question intonation*
What does the Canadian flag look like?
Do you know what the Olympic flag looks like?
Go to page 90.

LISTENING

1. Listen and complete this conversation.

A Do you know what this symbol means?
B Yes. It means _____.
A How do you spell that?
B _ _ _ _ _ _ _ _ _ _.
A What does it mean?
B It means that something can catch fire—like gasoline. Gasoline is _____.
A Oh, I see. Thanks.

2. What do these symbols mean? Listen and write the answer under each symbol. Then compare answers with your classmates.

a. _____

b. _____

c. _____

SHARE INFORMATION

1. Person A: Go to page 81.
   Person B: Go to page 82.

2. *Pairs*. Which signs are unfamiliar to you?
   Ask your partner about them.

Example:

Do you know what this sign means?

How do you say _____ in English?

How do you spell that?

Morocco

_____

South Africa

_____

Spain

_____

Australia

_____

Japan

_____

Jordan

_____

PREVIEW

1. *Pairs.* Look at the pictures and answer the questions below.

The way people wear their hair is often a symbol of something. Do you know why Buddhist monks shave their heads?

❑ To show they are very poor.
❑ To show that they have separated themselves from the world.
❑ To show that they live together.

Around the world weddings contain certain symbols. Do you know why brides in some countries paint their hands?

❑ To symbolize good luck.
❑ To represent the strength of love in marriage.
❑ To show that they are very rich.

The color black symbolizes different things in different cultures. Can you guess why these people are dressed in black?

❑ To show how important they are.
❑ To show that they are sad because someone has died.
❑ To show that they are in the same family.

2. Listen and check your guesses.

3. *Pairs.* Ask and answer these questions. Then share your answers with the class.

   a. In your country do any groups of people wear their hair in a special way? Why?
   b. In your country what are some symbols of love?
   c. In your country what does the color black symbolize?

READ AND TAKE NOTES

1. *Pairs.* Before reading the interview on page 11, answer these questions.

   a. What's the title of the interview?
   b. Do you know what "dreadlocks" are?
   c. Look quickly over the interview and study the pictures. Do you know what "dreadlocks" are now?

2. Read the interview on page 11 and <u>underline</u> the most important ideas.

Dreadlocks
Symbol of the "Natural Man" 🔊

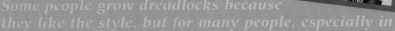

Some people grow dreadlocks because they like the style, but for many people, especially in Jamaica, dreadlocks are part of a way of thinking and living called Rastafarianism. Donovan Bonner, from Jamaica, recently talked to us about dreadlocks.

Interviewer: *Wow! Look at all that hair! How does it grow that way?*
Donovan: First, never comb the hair, and never, never cut the hair. Some people, for the first month, will put beeswax[1] on it. After that, just keep it natural and let it grow.

Interviewer: *Why do you wear dreadlocks?*
Donovan: Dreadlocks have been around a long, long time—centuries. In Jamaica, having dreadlocks means you're a Rastafarian. It means you believe a certain way.

A "Rasta-man" (or woman) is a "natural man." A Rasta-man doesn't eat red meat, drink alcohol, coffee, or milk. Many Rastafarians are vegetarians.[2] We know our roots lie in Africa.[3] A Rasta-man studies the Bible and meditates. Reggae music—Bob Marley music—helps us to do this. Hair is the foundation of[4] the natural man.

Interviewer: *How do you take care of dreadlocks?*
Donovan: We wash the hair only with special shampoo from the tuna plant (a cactus). Some people take a piece of this plant and slice it open. Inside is some stuff—it feels slimy[5]—that they put on the hair to help it grow. And sometimes they put the hair in a hat called a dread bag to take care of the locks and protect them from dirt.

[1]**beeswax:** wax made by bees
[2]**vegetarians:** people who don't eat meat
[3]**our roots lie in Africa:** our history started in Africa
[4]**the foundation of:** the most important part about being
[5]**slimy:** unpleasantly wet and slippery

3. *Pairs.* Read the article again and look for information to complete the chart below. Then compare answers with another pair.

Topic	Details
Dreadlocks	*they are never cut or combed*
Rastafarians	*people who believe in a certain way* *don't eat red meat*

TRUE OR FALSE?

1. *Pairs.* Write four sentences about dreadlocks or Rastafarians.

   Example:
   Many Rastafarians are vegetarians.

   a. _____
   b. _____
   c. _____
   d. _____

2. Change <u>two</u> of your sentences to make them false.

   Example:
   All
   ~~Many~~ *Rastafarians are vegetarians.*

3. Get together with another pair and read them your sentences. Ask them to identify the false sentences.

PUZZLE

Without looking back at page 11, complete the puzzle. If you don't know an answer, ask a classmate for help.

Example:
Do you remember how long dreadlocks have been around?
Do you know where Donovan Bonner is from?

ACROSS

3 Dreadlocks have been around for
  _____. *(how long?)*

4 Donovan Bonner is from
  _____. *(where?)*

7 Bob Marley played _____
  music. *(what kind of?)*

8 Rastafarians _____ comb their hair.
  (how often?)

9 Some people put _____ on their
  dreadlocks during the first month. *(what?)*

DOWN

1 Rastafarians avoid eating _____. *(what?)*

2 The shampoo for dreadlocks comes from
  the _____ _____. *(where?)*

5 Rastafarians refuse to drink _____. *(what?)*

6 Rastafarians sometimes use a _____
  _____ to protect their hair. *(what?)*

10 The tuna plant feels _____ inside. *(how?)*

Topic: **Men and Women**
Language: **Describing differences**
Focus: **Comparative adjectives and adverbs**

PRESENTATION

1. Do you think these statements are true or false?
   Put a check (✓) next to your answers.

	I think that's true.	I don't think that's true.
a. Women live longer than men.		
b. Women are more talkative than men.		
c. Men smile more often than women.		
d. Baby girls start talking earlier than baby boys.		
e. Men have better hearing than women.		

2. Listen and <u>underline</u> the words you hear.

Here's what researchers have found ...

a. Throughout the world, a woman's life expectancy is (*longer/shorter*) than a man's.

b. At meetings and social gatherings, women speak (*more often/less often*) than men. In public, women also speak for (*longer/shorter*) periods of time.

c. Beginning in their preteen years, men smile (*more often/less often*) than women.

d. In general, girls start talking (*earlier/later*) than boys. Girls also develop (*larger/smaller*) vocabularies.

e. Throughout life, a woman's hearing is (*better/worse*) than a man's. As babies, girls are (*more sensitive to/less sensitive to*) sounds, particularly their mother's voice.

Compare answers with your classmates.

PRACTICE

1. Read sentences *a–j* below. Then answer the questions at the bottom of the box.

> **DESCRIBING DIFFERENCES:**
> *Comparative Adjectives*
> a. In general, men are **taller than** women.
> b. At meetings, men are **more talkative than** women.
> c. At meetings, women are **less talkative than** men.
> *Comparative Adverbs*
> d. Women smile **more often than** men.
> e. Men smile **less often than** women.
> f. In general, men run **faster than** women.
> **not as + *adjective/adverb* + as**
> g. In general, women are **not as tall as** men.
> h. At meetings, women are **not as talkative as** men.
> i. Men do **not** smile **as often as** women.
> j. In general, women **cannot** run **as fast as** men.

> **NOTICE:**
> Men are taller than women. = Women are not as tall as men.
> Women smile more often than men. = Men do not smile as often as women.

- What's the comparative form of these adjectives: *tall, short, talkative, sensitive?*
- What's the comparative form of these adverbs: *often, frequently, fast?*

Answers on page 95

2. Restate the information in the sentences below. Then compare sentences with a partner.

a. In public, men speak more often than women.
In public, women don't speak as often as men.
In public, women speak less often than men.

b. In general, men are more muscular than women.
_____
_____

c. Men are more sensitive to bright lights than women.
_____
_____

d. In general, women gesture more quickly than men.
_____
_____

e. Research shows that a woman's brain ages more slowly than a man's.
_____
_____

f. Studies shows that men are more aggressive than women.
_____
_____

PRONUNCIATION POINT: Linked sounds

In general, men are taller than women.
Go to page 90.

LISTENING

1. Read the information below about men and women. Guess the missing words. Then listen and check your guesses.

Questions

a. On average, _____ live five to ten years longer than _____. Why do you think this is so?

b. In many places, a _____'s haircut is much more expensive than a _____'s. Why is this?

c. Throughout the world, most politicians are _____. Very few _____ hold important positions in government. What reasons can you give to explain this?

d. In most countries, elementary school teachers are usually _____, but university professors are usually _____. Why do you think this is so?

2. *Pairs.* We asked someone the questions above. How do you think she answered? Match her answers with our questions.

Answers

___ For one thing, I think it's a high-status job and men usually get those jobs.

___ Maybe it's because women are fussier than men.

___ I think it's because men aren't as patient as women.

_a_ One reason might be that men smoke more than women.

Listen and check your ideas.

WHAT DO YOU THINK?

1. *Groups.* Choose one of the questions above. Together come up with five possible answers of your own.

Example:
We think it's because …
Well, for one thing …
Maybe it's because …
One reason might be that …

Question:
1.
2.
3.
4.
5.

2. Present your group's ideas to the class.

PREVIEW

1. Listen and complete the questions below. Then listen again and check (✓) the answers you hear.

Questions	Answers
a. Do you think it's _____ for both the husband and wife to work outside the home?	☐ Sure. Why not? ☐ I think it depends. ☐ Absolutely not!
b. Do you think it's _____ for the mother or father to stay home with the children?	☐ The mother. ☐ The father. ☐ I don't think it matters.
c. Do you think fathers should spend as _____ time with the children as mothers?	☐ Sure. Why not? ☐ Absolutely not! ☐ No way!

Pairs. Take turns asking and answering the questions.

2. Choose one of these questions and interview five classmates. Record their answers in the chart below.

a. Do you think women should do all the cooking at home?
b. Do you think both parents should discipline the children?
c. Do you think men should know how to sew?
d. Do you think men should do as much housework as women?
e. Do you think a wife should wait on her husband?

Example:
Ⓐ Do you think women should do all the cooking at home?
Ⓑ No way!

Name	Yes	No	It depends.	Reason
1.	☐	☐	☐	
2.	☐	☐	☐	
3.	☐	☐	☐	
4.	☐	☐	☐	
5.	☐	☐	☐	

3. Report the results of your survey to the class.

Example:
I asked the question …
Three people said "yes" and two people said "no."

4. These household tasks appear in the poem below. Who do you think should do these things: the husband, the wife, or both?

shovel the walk   sew holey socks   rake up the leaves

READ AND RESPOND

1. *Pairs.* Listen as your teacher reads the following poem.

My Rules

If you want to marry me, here's what you'll have to do:
You must learn how to make a perfect chicken-dumpling stew.[1]
And you must sew my holey socks,
And you must soothe my troubled mind,[2]
And develop the knack for[3] scratching my back,
And keep my shoes spotlessly shined.
And while I rest you must rake up the leaves,
And when it is hailing and snowing
You must shovel the walk ... and be still[4] when I talk,
And—hey—where are you going?

    —Shel Silverstein

[1] chicken-dumpling stew: a kind of thick soup made with chicken
[2] soothe my troubled mind: help me to stop worrying
[3] develop the knack for: learn how to
[4] be still: be quiet

2. Take turns reading lines from the poem with a partner.

3. *Pairs.* Work together to answer these questions. Then report your answers to the class.

  a. Do you think the speaker of the poem is a man or a woman? Why?

  b. Would you want to marry this person? Why or why not?

SHARE IDEAS

1. *Pairs.* Think of different ways to complete these lines from the poem on page 17.

   a. If you want to marry me you must …

   > *cook me delicious meals.*
   > *rub my back every night.*
   > *tell me you love me every day.*

   _____

   _____

   _____

   b. When it is …, you must …

   > *When it is time to get up, you must bring*
   > *me breakfast in bed.*
   > *When it is cold outside, you must serve me hot tea.*

   _____

   _____

   _____

2. *Pairs.* Use your ideas from Activity 1 to write your own poem.

My Rules

If you want to marry me, here's what you'll have to do:

You must _____.

And you must _____,

And _____,

And _____,

And _____.

And _____,

And when it is _____

You must _____,

And—hey—where are you going?

3. Get together with another pair and take turns reading your poems aloud.

Strategy Session One

KEEPING A CONVERSATION GOING: ASKING QUESTIONS

1. *Pairs.* If you want to keep a conversation going, it helps to ask follow-up questions. Read the conversations below and try to guess the missing words. Then listen and write the words you hear.

a.   **A** Do you know what the smallest country in Asia is?
    B Yes. It's Nauru. It's a small island in the Pacific Ocean.
    A Nauru? I've never heard of it. _____*Where*_____ _____*is*_____ _____*it*_____ exactly?
    B It's about halfway between Australia and Hawaii.
    A I see. _____ _____ _____ _____?
    B It's very small—only about 21 square kilometers.
    A And _____ _____ _____ _____ Nauru?
    B Only about 9,000.
    A Wow! That *is* small!

b.   **A** Have you ever read any poetry in English?
    B Yes. I just finished a book of poems by Shel Silverstein.
    A Really? _____ _____ _____ _____?
    B *Where the Sidewalk Ends.*
    A And _____ _____ _____ _____?
    B I loved it. I thought it was very funny. You should read it.

Now practice the conversations with a partner.

2. What follow-up questions could you ask to keep these conversations going?

a.   **A** Do you have any brothers or sisters?
    B Yes. I have a younger sister.
    A _*What's her name?*_

b.   **A** When did you last buy a gift for someone?
    B Last Christmas.
    A _____?

c.   **A** How was your weekend?
    B Pretty good, thanks.
    A _____?

d.   **A** Have you ever stayed up all night?
    B Yes. I was studying for a test.
    A _____?

Compare ideas with your classmates.

3. Practice asking and answering the questions in Activity 2. Ask follow-up questions to keep your conversations going.

KEEPING A CONVERSATION GOING: EXPANDING YOUR ANSWERS

🔊 1. Listen to these two conversations. Then answer the questions below.

①

Ⓐ How was your weekend?
Ⓑ It was okay.
Ⓐ Did you do anything special?
Ⓑ No, not really.
Ⓐ Well, did you go anywhere?
Ⓑ Uh-huh.

②

Ⓐ How was your weekend?
Ⓑ It was okay. I didn't do anything special, but I heard some great music on the radio.
Ⓐ Really? What was it?
Ⓑ Zydeco music. It's a type of American music. It has a blues and French-Caribbean influence.
Ⓐ Interesting!

- How is the second conversation different from the first?
- In the first conversation, Person B gives only short answers. What effect does this have on the conversation?
- In the second conversation, Person B expands his answers. What effect does this have on the conversation?

2. Read each question below and answer *Yes* or *No*. Then give more information to expand your answer.

a. Do you watch sports on TV?
   No, not very often. I'd rather play a sport than watch it on TV.

b. Do you listen to the radio very often?
   _____

c. Did you go out last night?
   _____

d. Are there any good programs on TV?
   _____

e. Would you like to travel to another country?
   _____

3. *Pairs*. Take turns asking the questions below. Then try to keep your conversations going by asking more questions and expanding your answers.

   Did you take a vacation last year?

   Have you ever had a part-time job?

   What's your favorite sport?

   Have you ever been to a wedding?

   Do you think husbands should help with the housework?

Topic: Accidents
Language: Narrating
Focus: Past continuous and simple past

PRESENTATION

1. *Pairs*. Take turns asking and answering the questions below.

Are you afraid of lightning?

LIGHTNING

What should you do during a lightning storm? What shouldn't you do?

Have you ever been outside during a lightning storm? How did you feel?

Do you know of anyone who was hit by lightning? What happened?

2. Use the words in the box to complete the story below.

car	eyebrow	7
fishing	getting out of	71
lookout tower	shoulder	

HIT BY LIGHTNING
(A TRUE STORY)

Roy Sullivan was hit by lightning not just once but a total of __7__ times—in 1942, 1969, 1970, 1972, 1973, 1976, and 1977. The first time lightning hit Sullivan, he was working in a _____ in a U.S. National Park. Then 27 years later, lightning hit Sullivan again. This time he was driving his _____. Another time, lightning struck Sullivan while he was _____ his truck. And another time Sullivan was _____ when lightning struck him.

Sullivan was never seriously injured by lightning, but he did lose an _____ and a toenail. He was also burned on his _____, stomach, chest, and legs. "Lightning just has a way of finding me," Sullivan once said. Sullivan died in 1983 at the age of _____, but his death had nothing to do with lightning.

3. Compare ideas with a partner. Then listen and check your answers.

PRACTICE

1. Read sentences *a–d* and complete the chart. Then answer the questions at the bottom of the box.

> **NARRATING:** *Past continuous and simple past*
> a. Sullivan **was working** in a lookout tower when lightning **hit** him in 1942.
> b. Sullivan **was fishing** when lightning **hit** him in 1977.
> c. Another time, lightning **hit** Sullivan while he **was getting** out of his truck.
> d. Last year lightning **hit** eight people while they **were playing** golf.
>
> There are two actions in each of the sentences above. Group these actions in the chart below.
>
> | Incompleted or Interrupted Actions | Sudden Actions |
> |---|---|
> | a. *Sullivan was working* | *lightning hit him* |
> | b. _____ | _____ |
> | c. _____ | _____ |
> | d. _____ | _____ |
>
> - *Was working, was fishing, was getting,* and *were playing* are past continuous verbs. What kinds of actions do past continuous verbs describe?
> - Based on the examples above, how do you form the past continuous?
>
> **Answers on page 96**

2. Use the verbs in parentheses to complete each sentence. Then compare sentences with a classmate.

   a. I ___*cut*___ (cut) my finger while I ___*was making*___ (make) a sandwich.
   b. My brother _____ (hurt) his back while he _____ (play) tennis.
   c. I _____ (burn) my finger while I _____ (cook) dinner.
   d. My teacher _____ (sprain) his ankle while he _____ (play) basketball.
   e. My friend _____ (ride) a horse when she _____ (fall) and _____ (hit) her head.
   f. I _____ (walk) to school when I _____ (slip) on the ice and _____ (break) my arm.
   g. My sister _____ (go) down an escalator when she _____ (fall) and _____ (hurt) her knee.

3. *Pairs.* Think of a way to complete each sentence. Then act out one of your sentences. Can your classmates guess what happened?

   a. I broke my leg while I _____.
   b. I bruised my arm while I _____.
   c. I hurt my arm while I _____.
   d. I hurt my back while I _____.
   e. I burned my finger while I _____.
   f. I sprained my ankle while I _____.

⊙⊙ PRONUNCIATION POINT: *Sentence stress*
Sullivan was fishing when lightning hit him.

Go to page 90.

LISTENING

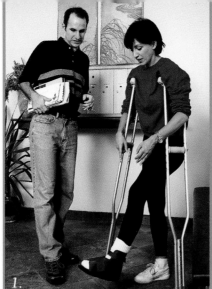

1. What happened to each person? Listen and check (✓) the statements you hear.

Ⓐ What did you do to your leg?
Ⓑ ❏ I sprained my ankle.
   ❏ I broke my ankle.
   ❏ I hurt my ankle.

Ⓐ Oh! How'd that happen?
Ⓑ ❏ I did it while I was playing basketball.
   ❏ I did it while I was playing volleyball.
   ❏ I did it while I was playing baseball.

Ⓐ That's too bad. When did it happen?
Ⓑ ❏ Last Tuesday.
   ❏ Last Wednesday.
   ❏ Last Thursday.

Ⓐ What happened to you?
Ⓑ ❏ I cut my hand.
   ❏ I cut my thumb.
   ❏ I cut my finger.

Ⓐ Really? How did you do it?
Ⓑ I was trying to _____ when my hand slipped.
   ❏ open a bottle with a knife
   ❏ open a box with a knife
   ❏ open a bag with a knife

Ⓐ Ouch! When did you do that?
Ⓑ ❏ Yesterday morning.
   ❏ Yesterday evening.
   ❏ Yesterday afternoon.

2. Practice the conversations with a partner.

GET THE DETAILS

1. Talk to different classmates. Find people who answer *Yes* to the questions below. Then ask more questions to get the details.

Example:
Ⓐ Have you ever broken a bone?
Ⓑ Yes, I have. I broke my arm when I was a kid.
Ⓐ How did you do it?
Ⓑ I was playing baseball.

Have you ever ...	Name	How? When? Where?
● broken a bone?		
● hurt your hand?		
● sprained an ankle?		
● been in a car accident?		
● gotten hurt while you were playing a sport?		

2. Tell the class about one person in your chart.

PREVIEW

1. *Pairs.* The pictures below show details from two amazing stories. Without reading the stories, can you guess what each story is about? Use the words in each box to help you.

caught on fire
fell
parachute
was flying

on the couch
rock
was sleeping
living room

2. *Pairs.* Report your ideas to the class.

Example:
In the first story, we think a plane caught on fire, then …

READ AND SHARE INFORMATION 📼

1. Read the first part of each story to check your predictions from page 24. Then think of three things you want to know about the rest of each story. Write your questions on the lines.

THE BURNING AIRPLANE

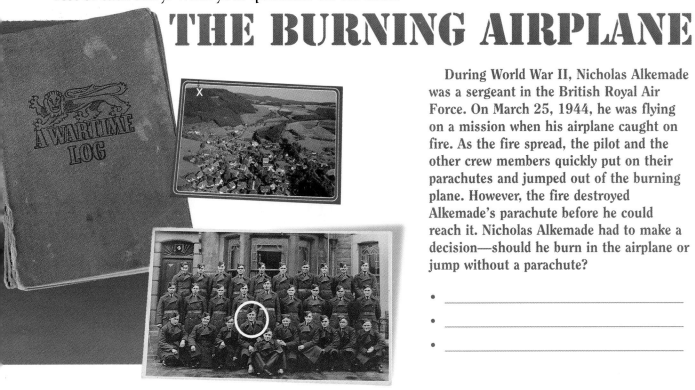

During World War II, Nicholas Alkemade was a sergeant in the British Royal Air Force. On March 25, 1944, he was flying on a mission when his airplane caught on fire. As the fire spread, the pilot and the other crew members quickly put on their parachutes and jumped out of the burning plane. However, the fire destroyed Alkemade's parachute before he could reach it. Nicholas Alkemade had to make a decision—should he burn in the airplane or jump without a parachute?

- _____
- _____
- _____

The Big Bang

Ann Hodges was a housewife in Sylacauga, Alabama, in the United States. On the afternoon of November 30, 1954, something very unusual happened to her. On that day, Mrs. Hodges was not feeling well and was taking a nap on the sofa in her living room. Suddenly, she was awakened by a loud bang and a sharp pain in her left hip. She looked around and noticed that there was a hole in her ceiling and that some of her furniture was broken.

- _____
- _____
- _____

2. *Pairs.* Find out how these stories end.
   Person A: Go to page 83.
   Person B: Go to page 84.

TELL A STORY

1. *Pairs.* Number the pictures to tell a story.
   Then tell your story to another pair. Use
   the words in the box to help you.

ambulance	tickle	sink
knock himself	ticklish	stretcher
unconscious	leak	husband
paramedics	plumber	wife

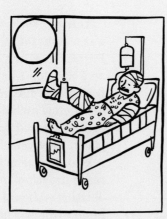

2. Listen to someone telling a story using the pictures
   in Activity 1. Is it the same as your story?

Topic: **People**
Language: **Emphasizing continuity**
Focus: **Present perfect continuous**

PRESENTATION

1. What would you like to find out about these people?
   Choose (✓) one question from each list.

Claudio Amaral is an ultralight pilot from Brasilia, Brazil.

❏ How long has he been flying?
❏ How did he learn how to fly an ultralight?
❏ Does he own his own ultralight?

Rosalie Warren is a student at Suffolk University in the U.S.

❏ How long has she been studying at Suffolk University?
❏ How old is she?
❏ What is she studying now?

Gemma Dickmann lives in Holland, where she collects pencil sharpeners.

❏ What does she do for a living?
❏ How long has she been collecting pencil sharpeners?
❏ How many pencil sharpeners has she collected?

2. Listen for the answers to the questions you chose.
   Then report what you learned to the class.

3. *Pairs.* Ask and answer these questions.

   a. Would you like to take flying lessons? Why or why not?
   b. Do you know an older person who is studying something? If so, what?
   c. Do you collect anything? If so, what?

PRACTICE

1. Read the conversations. Then answer the questions below.

EMPHASIZING CONTINUITY: *Present perfect continuous*

a. Interviewer: Where in the United States do you live?
Rosalie: In Boston.
Interviewer: Oh, yeah? How long **have** you **been living** there?
Rosalie: Over 20 years.

b. Interviewer: What do you do for a living?
Gemma: I work for the post office.
Interviewer: Really? How long **have** you **been doing** that?
Gemma: Oh, for about 25 years.

c. Interviewer: Do you own your own plane?
Claudio: Yes. I have a Fox V-II.
Interviewer: Really? How long <u>have</u> you <u>had</u> it?
Claudio: For about seven years.

• The **bold-faced** verbs are in the present perfect continuous tense. How do we form this tense?
• The <u>underlined</u> verb is in the present perfect simple. Some verbs do not have a continous form. *Have* when it means *own* is one of them. Can you think of any others?

Answers on page 97

2. *Pairs.* Complete the missing questions in these conversations.

a. **A** Who's that playing the guitar?
B That's my sister.
A She's pretty good! *How long has she been playing?* (*play*)
B Oh, for about five years.

b. **A** What's your cousin doing in Canada?
B She's studying international business.
A Really? _____ that? (*do*)
B Since last September.

c. **A** Where do you work?
B At Molita's. It's a restaurant downtown.
A Uh-huh. _____ there? (*work*)
B For a year or so.

d. **A** What do you do for a living?
B I'm a pilot. I work for British Airways.
A Really? _____ a pilot? (*be*)
B Since 1986.

e. **A** Is that your new car?
B Yes. Do you like it?
A Yes. It's nice. _____ it? (*had*)
B For just a week.

3. Listen and check your answers.

PRONUNCIATION POINT: *Reduced forms*
How long has Rosalie Warren been living in Boston?
How long have you been studying English?
Go to page 91.

LISTENING

1. Listen and complete the conversations.

FOR …

> 20 minutes   a month
> an hour   about a year
> a week   about 10 years

SINCE …

> lunch   April
> 8:00 A.M.   1997
> last week   I was a child

a. **A** Do you collect anything?
   B Well, I collect Snoopy toys. I have a huge collection.
   A Have you been collecting them for a long time?
   B Yes, _____.

b. **A** Do you play an instrument?
   B Yes. I play the flute, but not very well.
   A How long have you been playing?
   B _____.
   A Really? Wow! You must be pretty good.
   B Oh, no. Not really.

c. **A** Do you have any hobbies?
   B Well … I like to play around on my computer.
   A Really? How long have you had a computer?
   B _____.
   A Do you have e-mail?
   B Of course. I couldn't live without it.
   A How long have you been using it?
   B _____.

2. *Pairs.* Compare answers with a partner. Then practice the conversations.

INTERVIEW

1. Talk to different classmates. Find people who do the activities in the chart. Then ask questions to get more information.

Example:
A Do you collect something?
B Yes. Stamps.
A Really? How long have you been doing that?
B For about five years.

Find someone who …	Name	How long?	Additional information
a. collects something			
b. plays an instrument			
c. uses e-mail			
d. works somewhere			
e. has a pen pal			
f. plays on a sports team			

2. Tell about one of the people in your chart.

Example:
Yuko has been collecting stamps for about five years.

PREVIEW

1. *Groups.* Study the pictures below. Then work together to complete the chart.

Tadao Hiraoka is a Japanese painter who has been working on a special art project for more than 15 years.

What do you know about Tadao Hiraoka?	What would you like to find out about him?
He's a painter.	*Does he usually paint outdoors?*

Compare charts with your classmates.

2. *Groups.* Look at the pictures on page 31 and share ideas with your classmates.

   a. How are the two paintings alike? How are they different?
   b. What's your opinion of the paintings?

READ AND REPORT 🔲

1. Read the article below and look for answers to your questions on page 30.

1,600 GIANT TREES

One snowy morning 15 years ago, Tadao Hiraoka took a walk along the Tokai Nature Path. On this particular day, he was looking for a subject for a painting. "As I climbed to the Otome pass near Shojiko Lake—one of the five Mt. Fuji lakes—I came across a giant cedar tree. I was greatly moved."[1]

Hiraoka, now 65, has been painting giant trees ever since. Working mainly in watercolor and sumi,[2] he has created more than 1,600 paintings of giant trees.

"Although big trees appear strong, they are really quite delicate and are sensitive to small changes in the environment," says Hiraoka. "The old trees are representatives of the whole forest and act as environmental sensors. Many of the trees that I have drawn are now dead as a result of environmental degradation.[3] These are dangerous times for old trees."

In an effort to save Japan's giant trees, Hiraoka and a group of fellow tree-lovers have drawn a map showing where the trees are located. (Hiraoka defines a giant tree as one with a trunk greater than 5 meters in circumference at 1.3 meters above the ground.) The group has also developed a lightning rod for giant trees, and has produced postcards of Hiraoka's work to educate people about the plight of Japan's giant trees.[4]

Hiraoka says he hopes to complete 2,000 pictures of giant trees in his lifetime, and to paint trees growing outside Japan too.

[1] **was greatly moved:** felt strong emotions
[2] **sumi:** a special kind of Japanese black ink
[3] **environmental degradation:** the worsening of the environment
[4] **the plight of Japan's giant trees:** how Japan's giant trees are in danger

2. Share any answers you found with your classmates.

油山寺の天狗形　県指定天然記念物
静岡県袋井市村松

水宮神社の大欅　幹周7.50m／県指定天然記念物／群馬県藤岡市

ASK QUESTIONS

1. *Groups.* Here are the answers to some questions about Tadao Hiraoka. What do you think the questions are?

How old is he?		
65.	Giant trees.	Since he was 50.
	1,600.	2,000.

Listen to the questions and answers.

2. Write the answers to six questions about yourself. Include numbers in some of your answers. See if a classmate can guess the questions.

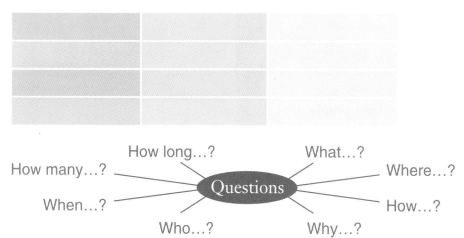

How long...?   What...?

How many...?   (Questions)   Where...?

When...?   How...?

Who...?   Why...?

GET THE DETAILS

1. Think of people who are doing interesting things. Write a sentence about each person on another piece of paper.

   Example:
   My sister teaches young children.
   A friend of mine restores old cars in his free time.

2. *Pairs.* Exchange papers with your partner. Choose one of your partner's sentences and write questions to get information about the person.

   Example:

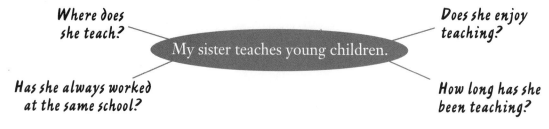

Where does she teach?   Does she enjoy teaching?

My sister teaches young children.

Has she always worked at the same school?   How long has she been teaching?

3. *Pairs.* Answer your partner's questions.

PRESENTATION

1. Choose a number from the box to complete each statement.

84	thousands of	72,135	2
100	3 1/2	50	

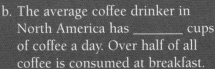

FOOD FACTS

a. A person who lives to age 72 and eats three times a day will eat _72,135_ meals during his or her lifetime.

b. The average coffee drinker in North America has _____ cups of coffee a day. Over half of all coffee is consumed at breakfast.

c. Honey is the only food that does not spoil. Honey from the Egyptian tombs still tastes very good, even though it is _____ years old.

d. Rice is the main food for _____ percent of the people in the world.

e. Apples are _____% water.

f. There are about 300,000 plants in the world, but only about _____ are grown and eaten on a regular basis.

g. Most healthy adults can live without food for about a month, but they must drink at least _____ liters of water a day to survive.

2. *Pairs.* Compare ideas with a partner.

Example:
Ⓐ I think a person who lives to age 72 will eat …
Ⓑ That sounds right. (Are you sure? I think …)

🔲 Listen and check your ideas.

PRACTICE

1. Match each description with a food on the right.

1. a sundae

2. thousand-year-old eggs

3. bi bim bap

> **DESCRIBING: *Present simple passive***
>
> __3__ a. This Korean dish **is made** with rice, vegetables, meat, and beans.
>
> ___ b. It **is** sometimes **topped** with a fried egg.
>
> ___ c. It **is made** with ice cream, chocolate sauce, whipped cream, and a red cherry on top.
>
> ___ d. They **are buried** for about eight weeks.
>
> ___ e. Chopped nuts **are** usually **sprinkled** on top.
>
> ___ f. They **are eaten** raw and taste somewhat fishy.
>
> • Look at the sentences above. Sentences *a–c* use *is*, but sentences *d–f* use *are*. Why?
>
> • Look back at page 33 and underline the passive verbs.
>
> Answers on page 98

2. *Pairs.* How are the foods below usually cooked? Write *often*, *sometimes*, or *never*.

Example:

Ⓐ Fish is often baked.

Ⓑ Right, and sometimes it's boiled. Is it ever stir-fried?

Ⓐ Sure. Often.

	Baked	Boiled (Simmered)	Stir-fried/ Sautéed	Deep-fried	Steamed	Barbecued/ Grilled
fish	*often*	*sometimes*	*often*			
onions						
rice						
potatoes						
carrots						
chicken						

Compare ideas with your classmates. Then add other foods to the chart.

LISTENING

1. We asked three people the questions below.
   Listen and put a check (✓) next to their answers.

What's one of your favorite dishes?

	Person 1 *sukiyaki*	Person 2 *feijoada*	Person 3 *crème caramel*
What is it?	☐ It's a kind of soup. ☐ It's a vegetable dish. ☐ It's a one-pot dish.	☐ It's a kind of stew. ☐ It's a vegetable dish. ☐ It's a kind of bread.	☐ It's a kind of soup. ☐ It's an appetizer. ☐ It's a dessert.
What's it made of?	☐ beef ☐ vegetables ☐ fish ☐ noodles	☐ potatoes ☐ milk ☐ black beans ☐ sausage	☐ onions ☐ milk ☐ apples ☐ eggs
How is it cooked?	☐ It's simmered. ☐ It's fried. ☐ It's broiled.	☐ It's baked. ☐ It's grilled. ☐ It's simmered.	☐ It's fried. ☐ It's baked. ☐ It's boiled.
What does it taste like?	☐ It's very spicy. ☐ It's a little sweet. ☐ It's bitter.	☐ It's spicy. ☐ It's mild. ☐ It's delicious.	☐ It's sour. ☐ It's sweet. ☐ It's salty.

2. Compare ideas with your classmates.

DESCRIBE

1. *Pairs.* Choose a dish you and your partner both like.
   Then answer these questions.

Dish: _____

a. What kind of dish is it?   *It's ...* _____
b. What's it made with?   _____
c. How is it cooked?   _____
d. What does it taste like?   _____

2. Read your answers aloud and ask your classmates
   to identify the dish.

Example:
It's a dessert.
It's made with apples.
It's baked.
It's a little sour.

🔊 PRONUNCIATION POINT: *Sentence intonation*
Bi bim bap is made with rice, vegetables, meat, and beans.
Go to page 91.

PREVIEW

1. *Pairs.* Take turns asking and answering the questions below. Record your partner's answers.

Questionnaire: Eating Out

a. When was the last time you ate out?	☐ last week ☐ two weeks ago	☐ three weeks ago ☐ more than a month ago	
b. Where did you go?			
c. How did you find out about this place?	☐ from a friend ☐ from a restaurant guidebook	☐ from a sign in front ☐ from an advertisement	☐ other:
d. What kind of food does it serve?	☐ French ☐ Chinese	☐ Italian ☐ Mexican	☐ other:
e. What was the ambience like?	☐ quiet and romantic ☐ fancy	☐ informal ☐ crowded and loud	☐ exotic
f. How was the service?	☐ friendly ☐ polite	☐ gracious ☐ fast	☐ slow ☐ unfriendly
g. How were the prices?	☐ very expensive ☐ expensive	☐ average ☐ cheap	
h. How was the food?	☐ excellent ☐ pretty good	☐ so-so ☐ disappointing	

Get together with another pair and report your partner's answers.

Example:
She said the last time she ate out was …
She went to …

2. Read the statements below about Tim and Nina Zagat.
Then listen and check (✓) *True* or *False*.

TIM and NINA ZAGAT publish these popular restaurant guides.

	True	False
a. In the late 1970s, Tim and Nina left New York to work as doctors in Paris, France.	___	___
b. While they were living in Paris, they collected a list of good restaurants in the city. They gave the list to their friends.	___	___
c. When the Zagats moved back to New York, they asked their friends to recommend good restaurants there. They put their friends' recommendations in a book and gave each friend a copy.	___	___
d. In 1992, they began selling their guidebook on restaurants in New York City.	___	___
e. Today, they publish 15 guidebooks on restaurants in different cities.	___	___

3. Listen again and correct the false statements.

READ AND IDENTIFY

1. Match the interviewer's questions with Tim and Nina Zagat's answers. Write the questions on the lines.

Interviewer's Questions

a. Are people eating out more often?
b. Do you have a favorite junk food?
c. Describe the most memorable meal you have ever eaten.
d. How do you judge a restaurant?
e. Would you like to own a restaurant?
f. Why did you create your restaurant guides?

Tim and Nina Zagat (an interview) 🔲

Tim: We were both working for law firms in Paris, and Nina was also attending the Cordon Bleu.[1]
Nina: We tried restaurants everywhere, and I kept a list of them for clients who wanted to know where to eat. So, in a way, that was our first guide.

a. Are people eating out more often?

Tim: Yes, since there are a greater number of women in the workplace, eating out is in.[2]
Nina: And taking out[3] is also in.

Nina: It was with four close friends at a restaurant near the Pont Neuf in Paris. We were cold and hungry when we stumbled upon[4] the place. There was a fire burning, and we ate fresh grilled lobster.

Nina: Really good hot dogs and cookies.
Tim: Pizza and Double Whoppers with cheese.

Tim: By smell—I don't like the aroma of cleaning products; by sight—the ambience and the decor; by service.
Nina: And, of course, by the presentation[5] and the taste of the food.

Tim & Nina: No!

[1] **the Cordon Bleu:** a famous cooking school in France
[2] **eating out is in:** eating in restaurants is popular now
[3] **taking out:** taking food out of a restaurant to eat at home
[4] **stumbled upon:** found by accident
[5] **the presentation (of the food):** the way the food is served

2. *Pairs.* Take turns asking and answering these questions.

a. How do the Zagats judge a restaurant? What about you?
b. What's their favorite junk food? What's yours?
c. What was your most memorable meal?

LISTENING

1. We asked three people from Vancouver to recommend a good restaurant. Listen and write their answers in the chart below.

	Claire	Steve	Jenny
a. What's a good restaurant in Vancouver?	Tojo's	The Fish House	Sophie's Cosmic Cafe
b. What kind of food does it serve?			
c. What's the ambience like?			
d. How's the service?			
e. How are the prices?			

2. Which of the three restaurants sounds the most interesting to you? Would you like to go there? Why or why not? Tell a classmate.

WHAT'S YOUR RECOMMENDATION?

1. *Pairs.* What's a good restaurant in your area? Ask your partner the questions below and record his or her answers.

Your partner's answers

a. What's a good restaurant near you? _____
b. Where is it? _____
c. What kind of food does it serve? _____
d. What's the ambience like? _____
e. How's the service? _____
f. How are the prices? _____
g. What do you like best about this place? _____

2. *Pairs.* Get together with a new partner. Tell him or her about the restaurants you and your first partner talked about.

Strategy Session Two

KEEPING A CONVERSATION GOING: AGREEING

1. *Pairs.* Below are some ways you can agree with affirmative statements. Listen to the conversations and add the missing words.

> So am I.   I am too.   Me too.
> So do I.   I do too.
> So was I.   I was too.
> So did I.   I did too.
> So would I.   I would too.

a. **A** Have you ever tried Indonesian food?
   B No, I haven't. But I'd love to someday.
   A *So would I*. It looks delicious!

b. **A** I love reggae music.
   B _____. Have you ever heard of Horace Andy?
   A No, I haven't. Is he any good?
   B Yeah. He's great!

c. **A** Have you ever broken a bone?
   B Yeah. I broke my wrist a few years ago while I was skating.
   A Really? _____. Three years ago.

d. **A** I liked that story about Nicholas Alkemade.
   B _____. It was unbelievable!

Now practice the conversations with your partner.

2. *Pairs.* Below are some ways you can agree with negative statements. Listen to the conversations and add the missing words.

> Neither am I.   I'm not either.   Me neither.
> Neither do I.   I don't either.
> Neither was I.   I wasn't either.
> Neither did I.   I didn't either.
> Neither would I.   I wouldn't either.

a. **A** Are you going anywhere over the vacation?
   B No, I don't think so. I don't have any money.
   A _____. Oh, well.

b. **A** I wouldn't want to fly in an ultralight.
   B _____. They're much too small.

c. **A** Do you like to try new foods?
   B No, not really. I'm not very adventurous.
   A _____.

d. **A** I didn't do my homework last night.
   B Uh-oh. _____!

Now practice the conversations with your partner.

KEEPING A CONVERSATION GOING: DISAGREEING POLITELY

1. *Pairs.* Below are some ways people can politely disagree.
   Listen to the conversations and add the missing words.

> Really? Why is that?   You do? Why is that?
> Really? Why not?   You don't? Why is that?
> Really? How come?   Really? I'd rather …
> Do you really think so?

a. **A** I don't like this food very much.
   B _____? _____ _____ _____?
   A It's too spicy.

b. **A** What! Corn on pizza! That's disgusting!
   B _____ _____ _____ _____ _____?
   I kind of like it.

c. **A** I love to eat out.
   B _____ _____ _____ _____ _____ _____.
   It's cheaper.
   A That's true. But it's more fun to eat out.

d. **A** I don't think I would recommend this restaurant to anyone.
   B _____? _____ _____?
   A The service is slow.
   B Yeah, but the food is good and it's cheap.

Now practice the conversations with your partner.

2. Listen to these people. Do they agree or disagree?
   Circle your answers.

   a. They agree.   They disagree.   d. They agree.   They disagree.
   b. They agree.   They disagree.   e. They agree.   They disagree.
   c. They agree.   They disagree.   f. They agree.   They disagree.

3. Ask and answer the questions below. See if your partner agrees
   or disagrees with you. Then ask questions and expand
   your answers to keep your conversations going.

   Example:
   A Did you like the story about the man who paints trees?
   B Yes, I did. I thought it was very interesting.
   A Me too. I liked …

   a. Did you like the story about the man who paints trees?
   b. Do you think that men and women should share the housework?
   c. Do you believe the story about Nicholas Alkemade?
   d. Would you like to run your own restaurant?
   e. Are you afraid of lightning?

Topic: **Inventions**
Language: **Describing**
Focus: **Simple past passive**

PRESENTATION

1. Where were these things invented? Match each
   item with a description below.

vacuum cleaner

toothpaste

traffic signal

contact lenses

sunglasses

bicycle

a. ___*Toothpaste*___ was invented 4,000 years ago by the Egyptians.
   They made it out of vinegar and ground stone.

b. The _____ was invented in France in 1790. The first one was
   made of wood, and it didn't have any pedals.

c. The first _____ was built in 1923 in the United States. It was a
   long pole with red and green signs on it. The red signs said "stop" and the
   green signs said "go."

d. The first _____ were worn by judges in China. Wearing them
   made it difficult to see a judge's eye expressions in court.

e. The first _____ was built in England in the 19th century. It was so big
   that it had to be pulled from house to house by horses.

f. The first _____ were developed by a Swiss doctor. They were thick
   and not very comfortable.

🔲 2. Listen and check your ideas.

PRACTICE

1. When do you think these things happened?
   Choose a year from the list on the right.
   Then listen and check your guesses.

> **DESCRIBING:** *Simple past passive*
>
> a. The first photograph **was taken** in _____.   • 1285
> b. Eyeglasses **were** first **worn** around _____.   • 1603
> c. Compact discs **were** first **marketed** in _____.   • 1826
> d. The telescope **was invented** in _____.   • 1832
> e. The first Sony Walkman **was sold** in _____.   • 1957
> f. The first satellite **was launched** in _____.   • 1979
> g. Matches **were** not **invented** until _____.   • 1982
>
> • Look at the **bold-faced** verbs above. When do we use *was*?
>   When do we use *were*?
> • How many examples of the simple past passive can you
>   find on page 41?
> **Answers on page 99**

2. *Pairs*. Work together to answer these questions.
   Circle your answers.

Example:
   (A) Do you know where the first basketball game was played?
   (B) I think it was in the United States. What do you think?
   (A) Me too. (Are you sure? I think ...)

a. Where was the first basketball game played?
   England/the United States/Russia

b. When was the electric iron invented?
   1882/1922/1942

c. Where was the printing press invented?
   China/the United States/Germany

d. Where were chairs first used?
   England/Egypt/France

e. When was color TV invented?
   1928/1948/1968

f. What were the first artificial eyes made of?
   glass/plastic/wood

g. When was the first X-ray photograph taken?
   1495/1895/1945

h. Where was the first typewriter made?
   the United States/Japan/India

Listen and check your answers.

PRONUNCIATION POINT: *Final - ed*

/ɪd/	/d/	/t/
invented	used	developed

Go to page 91.

LISTENING

1. Listen and add the missing information to the chart.

Invention	When was it invented?	Where was it invented?	Description (What was it like?)
The hot-air balloon			It was made of _____ and the inside was lined with _____ . On it's first trip, it rose to _____ meters.
The submarine			It was made of _____ and leather. It was rowed under water by _____ people.

2. *Pairs.* Compare charts with your partner.

SHARE INFORMATION

1. *Pairs.* Person A: Look at this page.
   Person B: Go to page 85.

2. Person A: Ask your partner questions to complete the chart below. Then use your chart to answer your partner's questions.

Example:
Ⓐ Do you know when aspirin was invented?
Ⓑ Yes. It was invented in 1853.

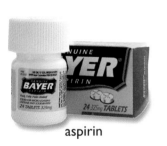
aspirin

fireworks

ink

the zipper

Invention	Where?	When?	Description
Aspirin	France		It was made from the bark (the outside part) of a tree.
Fireworks		a thousand years ago	They were used to scare away evil spirits.
Ink		about 4,500 years ago	The first ink was made of soot, _____, and plant material.
The zipper	The United States		The first zipper was used on a pair of boots.

3. *Pairs.* Use your charts to answer these questions.

a. Which invention is the oldest?
b. Which invention do you think is the most useful? Why?

PREVIEW

1. *Groups.* Match each description with one or more of the devices in *a–d*. Write the letter of the device.

pulley   spring   rope

Descriptions
___ You can fold it up.
___ It uses one or more pulleys.
___ It has a spring.
___ Large animals are used to pull the rope.
___ The driver pulls the rope.
___ It's made of cardboard.
___ You can hold it in your hand.

a.

b.

c.

d.

2. *Groups.* What is the purpose of each device? Agree on one answer for each device.

   Example:
   We think the purpose of device "a" is to ...

3. Go to page 86 and match each device with a description.

READ AND REPORT ☐

1. Look at the questions in the chart. Then read the article to find answers.

Questions	Answers
a. What problem did inventor Abraham Levy want to solve?	
b. Was Levy able to solve this problem easily?	
c. How were Levy's shades different from the earlier ones?	

A CHEAP & SIMPLE SOLUTION

Car windshield shades that look like giant sunglasses were invented by Abraham Levy of Israel. Over a million were sold in Israel from the mid-1970s to the mid-1980s. The idea came to Levy[1] when he had to park his car in the sun. He knew his car would be hot inside when he came back. He decided to invent something to solve the problem, but the first models didn't work. For instance, he tried products made of plywood, but they were not practical. Levy worked with lots of models and materials before he came up with folding cardboard.

The idea of windshield shades wasn't new with Levy. People before him had tried to make them. Some shades had folding legs and suction cups. Others rolled down. The earliest shade, invented in 1912, had curtains. But Levy's was the model that caught on.[2] It was simple, easy to use, and cheap—and people were willing to buy it.

So to be an inventor, you don't have to know a lot of math and science. Having an open mind[3] is more important. So is being willing to keep trying.

[1] The idea came to Levy: Levy thought of the idea
[2] caught on: became popular
[3] Having an open mind: Being willing to consider new ideas

2. Look at the article again and find a synonym for these words.

Synonyms

a. very large (paragraph 1) _____
b. returned (paragraph 1) _____
c. weren't successful (paragraph 1) _____
d. for example (paragraph 1) _____
e. the first (paragraph 2) _____
f. inexpensive (paragraph 2) _____

3. *Pairs.* Work together to answer these questions.

a. Do you agree that an inventor needs to have an open mind? Why or why not?
b. Think of an inventor you have heard about. What did this person invent? How would you describe this person?

SOLVE A PROBLEM

1. *Groups.* **Choose one of these problems**
   or think of one of your own.

   a. "When I wear earrings, they sometimes fall off and I
      lose one of them."
   b. "I'm always losing my umbrella. When I'm not using it,
      I'm always leaving it somewhere."
   c. "I have trouble getting up in the morning. I use an alarm clock,
      but I can't stop myself from turning it off and going back to sleep."
   d. "I'm always late because I can't find my keys. I can never find
      them when I'm in a hurry."
   e. "When I watch TV, the remote control always disappears.
      It takes me forever to find it."

2. *Groups.* **Think of different ways to solve the problem.**

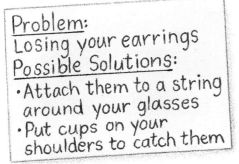

Problem:
Possible Solutions:

3. **Choose one solution. Draw a picture of it or describe**
   it in words. Then present your solution to the class.

Topic: **Mysterious things**
Language: **Reporting**
Focus: **Wh- words in statements**

PRESENTATION

1. What questions come to mind when you look at these pictures? List them below the pictures.

a.

b.

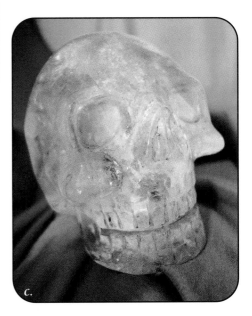

c.

What are they?
_____   _____   _____
_____   _____   _____
_____   _____   _____

2. Match each picture with a description below.
   Write the letter of the picture.

____

Hundreds of these round stones were found in Costa Rica in the 1930s. Some of the stones are huge—about 2.5 meters in diameter. Scientists have studied these stones for many years, but they still don't know who placed them there or why.

____

This skull was discovered in Mexico. It was carved out of crystal and is the same size as a human skull. Scientists believe that it was made about 1,000 years ago. However, they have not yet figured out how the skull was made or what its purpose was.

____

About 320 km south of Lima, Peru, there are some very strange lines on the ground. Made about 1,500 years ago, they are called the Nazca Lines. From the ground they look like ordinary lines, but from the air they form giant pictures. One group of lines, for example, forms a picture of a giant monkey. (One of the monkey's hands is over 12 meters across!) Nobody knows for sure why the Nazca people made these huge pictures.

3. Read the descriptions again and underline any answers to your questions from Activity 1.

PRACTICE

1. Read sentences *a–d* below and check (✓) *True* or *False*.

Answers on page 100

REPORTING: Wh- *words in statements*	True	False
a. Scientists don't know why the skull on page 47 was made.	✓	☐
b. Scientists haven't figured out what the skull is made of.	☐	☐
c. On page 47 it doesn't say where the skull was found.	☐	☐
d. Nobody can tell us how the skull was made.	☐	☐

- Circle the *wh-* word in each sentence. Which comes first after the *wh-* word—the subject or verb?

Answers on page 100

2. *Pairs.* What do we know about the Nazca Lines? What don't we know? Group these ideas in the chart below.

where they are	why they were made	who made them
how big they are	when they were made	what they look like
how many there are	how they were made	how long it took to make them

Things we know	Things we don't know
We know where they are.	*We don't know why they were made.*

Compare ideas with your classmates.

3. *Pairs.* Use the information on page 47 to complete the sentences about the round stones in Costa Rica.

a. We'll probably never know _____.

b. No one knows _____.

c. On page 47 it doesn't say _____.

d. Scientists haven't yet discovered _____.

e. No one is sure _____.

4. Read your sentences to a classmate. See if your classmate agrees with you.

PRONUNCIATION POINT: *Sentence stress*

We don't know why the Nazca Lines were made.

Go to page 91.

LISTENING

1. *Pairs.* Use the sentences in the box to make a conversation.

  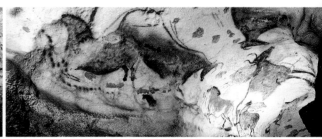

- Do you know what museum these paintings are in?
- That's amazing! Does anyone know who painted them?
- In a cave? You mean underground?
- No. No one knows. It's a total mystery.
- That's right. These horses were drawn on the wall of a cave in France.
- Yes. They were painted about 17,000 years ago.
- They're not in a museum. They're in a cave.
- Wow! Are they old?

Ⓐ *Do you know what museum these paintings are in?*
Ⓑ _____
Ⓐ _____
Ⓑ _____
Ⓐ _____
Ⓑ _____
Ⓐ _____
Ⓑ _____

2. Listen and check your answers.

3. *Pairs.* What would you like to know about the Bratton Horse? Share ideas with your partner.

Example:
I'd like to know …
I'd be interested in knowing …
I wonder …

4. Listen for answers to the questions below about the Bratton Horse and take notes.

The Bratton Horse was carved into the side of a chalky hill.

Questions	Answers
1. What country is the Bratton Horse in?	1.
2. How big is it?	2.
3. How old is it?	3.
4. How was it made?	4.
5. Who made it?	5.

5. Use your notes to complete this description.

The Bratton Horse was carved into the side of a hill in _____ more than _____ years ago. It's large—nearly _____ meters long. Unfortunately, no one knows for sure _____ or _____.

PREVIEW

1. *Pairs*. Look at the illustrations to the story "The Mysterious Box" and answer these questions.

   a. Do you know what the mysterious round box is?
   b. Can you tell how big the box is?
   c. Based on the pictures, what do you think the story is about?

   Compare ideas with your classmates.

2. Match the sentences below with the illustrations. Use context to guess the meaning of the bold-faced words.

   ___ For a moment Nasreddin didn't say anything. Then he did a most **amazing** thing. He started crying and laughing at the same time.

   ___ Nasreddin looked **intently** at the small strange box as the men showed it to him.

   ___ One day Nasreddin was walking through town when he **came across** a group of people.

   ___ When Nasreddin turned the box, the needle **quivered**. When the needle stopped moving, it was always pointing in the same direction.

3. *Pairs*. Use the illustrations and sentences above to make a chart like the one below.

The Mysterious Box	We know...	We don't know...
	what the man's name is	*who the other men are*

READ AND RESPOND

1. Look at the chart above. Then read the story to find the information you don't know.

The Mysterious Box

One day Nasreddin was walking through town when he came across a group of people with their heads together. They seemed to be looking at something on the ground. Nasreddin was curious to know what they were looking at, so he joined the group.

a.

"We're wondering what this strange thing is," a man by the name of Mustafa said to Nasreddin. "When Musa was coming into town, he found it on the road."

"Nobody knows what it is," Musa said.

b.

Nasreddin looked intently at the small round box of metal and glass. Inside the box he saw letters and a tiny needle that quivered as the box was turned. But it always came to rest pointing in the same direction.

"You know everything, Nasreddin." It was Mustafa speaking. "Can you tell us what it is?"

For a moment Nasreddin didn't say anything. Then he did a most amazing thing. First he cried and then he laughed. He repeated this again and again—crying and laughing, laughing and crying, crying and laughing.

"Why are you crying?" asked Musa.

"Why are you laughing?" asked Mustafa.

"Nobody should cry and laugh at the same time," said Musa. "What's wrong?"

c.

"I'll tell you why I am crying and why I am laughing," said Nasreddin. "I am crying," he began, "because not one of you knows what this little round box is. How stupid you are! Are you surprised that I cry?"

Nasreddin looked at the people gathered around him. Everyone looked down at the ground, even the little children, and for several minutes no one said anything. Finally Mustafa spoke up.

"You have told us why you are crying," Mustafa said. "Now tell us why you are laughing."

Nasreddin laughed once more.

"I am laughing," he said, "because I don't know what it is either!"

d.

2. Share any new information you found with your classmates.

3. Listen to the story and read along.

WHAT DO YOU THINK?

1. *Groups.* Work together to agree on answers
   to these questions.

   a. Why didn't Nasreddin tell the truth right away?
   b. Do you think Nasreddin is a smart man? Why or why not?
   c. On a scale of 1 (poor) to 10 (excellent), how would you rate this story? Why?

   Report your group's answers to the class.

2. **Look back at the story to find a synonym for each of
   these words or terms. Write them on the lines.**

	Synonyms
We'd like to know…	_____
very small	_____
unusual	_____
over and over; repeatedly	_____
What's the matter?	_____
dumb; not smart	_____

ROLE PLAY

1. *Groups of four.* **Follow these instructions to
   role-play the story "The Mysterious Box."**

   a. Choose one person to be the director.
   b. Decide who will play the characters in the story.
   c. Turn to pages 50–51 and <u>underline</u> your character's
      words in the story. Then practice reading
      them aloud. Follow your director's instructions.
   d. If you want you can add your own lines.

   CHARACTERS

    Nasreddin
    Mustafa
    Musa

   <u>Director</u>
   • Show the actors where to stand.
   • Make sure the actors use gestures and body language.
   • Help the actors practice their lines.

2. **Stand up and act out the story. Use gestures and
   body language. If time permits, change roles
   and act out the story again.**

Topic: **Rules and laws**
Language: **Giving opinions**
Focus: **Should + be + past participle + to; should + have to**

PRESENTATION

1. *Pairs.* What are the missing numbers in these sentences? Choose numbers from the list below and write them on the lines.

| 1 | 16 | 18 | 18 | 21 | 25 | 71 | 90 |

a. In Taiwan, a woman can't get married until she is _____ years old. A man has to be _____.

b. Girls in the United States weren't allowed to wear jeans to school until about _____ years ago.

c. _____ years ago, people didn't have to take a test to get a driver's license. Now they do.

d. Women in Switzerland weren't permitted to vote until 19____.

e. On the island of Bermuda people are not allowed to own more than _____ car.

f. In England you have to be _____ in order to drink alcohol. In the United States you have to be _____.

▭ Listen and check your ideas.

2. *Groups.* Work together to answer the questions below. Then report your group's ideas to the class.

What's your opinion?

a. Do you think students should be allowed to wear whatever they want to school?
b. At what age should people be allowed to get married?
c. Do you think people should have to take a test to get a driver's license?
d. Do you think people should be allowed to drink alcohol? Do you think there should be an age restriction?

PRACTICE

1. *Pairs.* Read sentences *a–f* below and check (✓)
I agree or *I disagree.*

GIVING OPINIONS: Should + be + *past participle* + to; should + have to

	I agree.	I disagree.
a. I don't think people **should be allowed** to smoke in restaurants.	❏	❏
b. I don't think people **should be allowed** to use cell phones in restaurants.	❏	❏
c. I think people **should be permitted** to own guns.	❏	❏
d. I think everyone **should have to** get married.	❏	❏
e. I don't think anyone **should have to** pay taxes.	❏	❏
f. In my opinion, children **shouldn't have to** go to school.	❏	❏

Look at the **bold-faced** verbs above.
- What is similar about the form of the verbs in sentences *a–c?*
- What is similar about the form of the verbs in sentences *d–f?*

Answers on page 101

2. Use the ideas below to write five opinions.

a. _____
b. _____
c. _____
d. _____
e. _____

I think I don't think	people anyone everyone children teenagers men women old people	should be allowed to watch TV. should be encouraged to quit smoking. should be allowed to get divorced. should be allowed to color their hair. should be permitted to stay up as late as they want. should be required to have full-time jobs. should have to do homework every night. should have to take a test to enter a university. should have to pay taxes. should have to help out at home.

Now read your opinions to a classmate. See if your
partner agrees or disagrees with you.

Example:

(**A**) I don't think children should
be allowed to watch TV.

(**B**) I don't think
so either.

(**B**) Really? Why is that?

(**A**) Because…

(**A**) I think everyone should
have to pay taxes.

(**B**) I think so too.

(**B**) Really? Why is that?

(**A**) Because…

🔊 PRONUNCIATION POINT: *Reduced forms*

/hævtə/

Do you think students should have to do homework every night?
Go to page 92.

LISTENING

1. We asked two people for their opinions.
   Listen and complete the questions below.

Survey Questions	Person 1			Person 2		
	Yes	No	I don't know.	Yes	No	I don't know.
a. Do you think people should _____ if they want to have children?	◡	◡	◡	◡	◡	◡
b. Do you think people should _____ as many children as they want?	◡	◡	◡	◡	◡	◡
c. Do you think people should _____ their children to school?	◡	◡	◡	◡	◡	◡

2. Listen again and record their answers in the chart above.
   Check (✓) *Yes, No,* or *I don't know.*

3. *Pairs.* Take turns asking and answering the questions.

SURVEY

1. What rules do students in your school have to
   follow? Add them to the chart.

have to / are required to	Students	aren't allowed to
do homework *take tests* *do what the teacher says*		*skip class* *smoke in school* *disrupt class*

   Now use the ideas in the chart to come up with opinion questions.

   Example:
   Do you think students should have to <u>do homework</u>?
   Do you think students should be required to <u>take tests</u>?
   Do you think students should be allowed to <u>skip class</u>?

2. *Pairs.* Choose <u>one</u> of the groups of people from the
   box at the right. Then make a chart like the one in
   Activity 1.

3. Use the ideas in your chart to write five
   opinion questions.

   Example:
   Do you think _____ should …?

4. Choose one of your opinion questions and interview
   your classmates. Then report the results.

doctors
professional athletes
politicians
parents
teachers
police officers
soldiers

PREVIEW

1. We asked a teenager about the rules he has to follow in his family. Listen and check (✓) *has to* or *doesn't have to*.

Rules	has to	doesn't have to
a. be home on weeknights by 10 P.M.	☑	☐
b. tell someone where he's going when he goes out	☐	☐
c. help with the housework	☐	☐
d. do his own laundry	☐	☐
e. help with the cooking	☐	☐
f. take care of a younger sister or brother	☐	☐
g. go to bed at a certain time	☐	☐
h. get up in the morning when he is told to	☐	☐

2. *Pairs.* What rules do you have to (or did you have to) follow in your family? Tell your partner. Then report to the class.

Example:
Ⓐ I have to be home on weeknights by 10 P.M.
Ⓑ So do I. (Really? I have to be home by 9:00.)

READ AND TAKE NOTES

1. *Groups.* Before you read the newspaper article on page 57, answer these questions.

   a. What is the title of the article?
      Why might a mother "go on strike" (refuse to do any housework)?
   b. Study the photograph and read the caption. What do you think the article is about?

2. What would you like to find out about Mrs. Tribout? Write three questions in the chart below.

3. Read the article on page 57 to find answers to your questions. (If you don't find an answer, write *It didn't say.*)

Mrs. Tribout refused to come down from the treehou[se] until her children agreed to behave better.

What do you want to know about Mrs. Tribout?	
Questions	Answers
1.	
2.	
3.	

Mom Goes on Strike

By Robert Berner

When Michelle Tribout went on strike, she was only hoping to get some respect from her children. Instead, she became an international media star.

It all began when a newspaper reporter walked by the Tribout house and saw Mrs. Tribout in a treehouse. She was telling her husband (on the ground below) that she wasn't coming down or cooking or cleaning until the kids started pitching in[1] and showing some gratitude.[2]

The next day the local newspaper published a photograph of Mrs. Tribout in the treehouse. Soon after that, film crews from five TV stations showed up. The BBC (British Broadcasting Corporation) called, and so did a radio station in Australia.

Why did she go on strike? According to Mrs. Tribout, the children — Misty, who is 15 years old; Joseph, 13; and Rachel, 7 — were fighting, talking back[3] and failing to get out of bed. The final straw came[4] when they didn't get up for breakfast — even after she made five trips upstairs to wake them up.

When her children came home from school that afternoon, they found their mom in the treehouse and a big note on the mailbox. It read:

ON STRIKE MOM!
No cooking, cleaning, doctoring, banking, or taxi service.
Out of order!

Mrs. Tribout's husband, Sonny, supported the strike. So the kids cooked dinner and came outside promising to

Michelle Tribout

be nice. But Mrs. Tribout didn't budge.[5]

Next, the children baked their mom's favorite brownies and wrote an agreement with the following rules of behavior:

> I. Pitch in whenever you see something needs to be done.
>
> II. Act your age, not like you are five.
>
> III. Don't smart off.[6]
>
> IV. Come when you are called.
>
> V. We are the kids, you are the parents.
>
> VI. Give and take on an equal basis.
>
> VII. Ask before you do something.
>
> VIII. Do not hit or hurt anybody.

The children presented the agreement at 11:30 p.m. A contract was reached at midnight, and Mrs. Tribout finally came down from the treehouse.

---

[1] **pitching in:** helping do work around the house
[2] **showing some gratitude:** saying "thank you" sometimes
[3] **talking back:** answering Mrs. Tribout rudely
[4] **The final straw came:** Mrs. Tribout finally decided to act when
[5] **Mrs. Tribout didn't budge:** Mrs. Tribout didn't change her mind or move
[6] **smart off:** talk rudely and disrespectfully

4. *Groups.* Compare your answers with your questions on page 56.

SHARE IDEAS

1. *Groups.* Write two true and two false sentences
   about the story on page 57. Have your classmates
   identify the false statements and correct them.

2. Work together to answer these questions. Then
   report your group's answers to the class.

   a. How did Mrs. Tribout get her children to change their behavior?
      Do you think this was a good way? Why or why not?
   b. Why do you think Mrs. Tribout's story was reported in the news?
   c. What are some more common ways for parents to discipline their children?
   d. What rules would <u>you</u> put in a contract between parents and children?

WHAT DO YOU THINK?

1. *Pairs.* Ask your partner the questions below. Use the
   follow-up questions to get more information.

A Do you think children should be allowed
to watch TV during the school week?

B Sure.
A Do you think they should be allowed
to watch as much TV as they want?
B _____

B No, I don't.
A Why not?
B _____

A Do you think children should be punished
if they get a bad grade in school?

B Yes, I do.
A How do you think they
should be punished?
B _____

B No, I don't.
A Why not?
B _____

A Do you think high school students should be allowed to date?

B Sure.
A Should their dating be limited to weekends?
B _____

B No, I don't.
A Why not?
B _____

2. *Pairs.* Work together to complete these questions.

   a. Do you think _____ should be allowed to _____?
   b. Do you think _____ should have to _____?

   Now get together with another partner and ask your
   questions. Be sure to ask follow-up questions.

   Example:
   A Do you think 16 year olds should be allowed to get married?
   B Sure.
   A Do you think they should have to have their parents' permission?
   B Yes, that's probably a good idea.

Strategy Session Three

KEEPING A CONVERSATION GOING: HESITATING

1. *Pairs.* You can use the expressions below when you need more time to answer a question. Listen to the conversations and write the missing expressions.

> Hmmm ...   It's hard to say ...
> Ummm ...   It depends ...
> Well ...   Let me think ...
> Good question ...   I'm not sure ...

a. Ⓐ Do you remember where the Nazca Lines are?
   Ⓑ *Hmmm. Let me think ...*. I think they're in Peru.
   Ⓐ Do you remember when they were made?
   Ⓑ _____. I think it was about a thousand years ago.

b. Ⓐ Do you think children should be given an allowance?
   Ⓑ An allowance? What's that?
   Ⓐ Spending money from their parents.
   Ⓑ Oh, OK ... _____. Sure. Why not?
   Ⓐ How much should they be given?
   Ⓑ _____. I guess it depends on how old the child is.

2. Answer these questions using the expressions from above. Write your answers on the lines.

a. Ⓐ What's the best restaurant in town?
   Ⓑ _____

b. Ⓐ Who is better with money—men or women?
   Ⓑ _____

c. Ⓐ What is the most important thing you own?
   Ⓑ _____

d. Ⓐ What was your favorite food when you were little?
   Ⓑ _____

e. Ⓐ Who did you admire when you were growing up?
   Ⓑ _____

3. Take turns asking and answering the questions from Activity 2. Be sure to expand your answers and ask follow-up questions to keep your conversations going.

KEEPING A CONVERSATION GOING: GROUP WORK

1. You will hear parts of three different group discussions. What are these students talking about? Listen and write the number of the discussion.

____ Solving an everyday problem.

____ Interesting experiences they have had.

____ What students should and shouldn't have to do.

2. When you're working in a group, it's important to encourage each other to keep talking. Read the expressions below. Then listen to the three discussions again and check (✓) the expressions you hear.

DISCUSSION 1
____ Oh, yeah?
____ Really?
____ Interesting!
____ Uh-huh.
____ No kidding!

DISCUSSION 2
____ Good idea!
____ Now *there's* an idea!
____ Uh-huh.
____ I like that idea!
____ Hmmm. I hadn't thought of that.

DISCUSSION 3
____ Good point!
____ That's true!
____ That's right.
____ I agree.
____ Uh-huh.

3. *Groups.* Choose <u>one</u> of the questions below and discuss it in your group. Be sure to encourage each other to keep talking.

a. Do you know any good restaurants? Which ones would you recommend and why?
b. What was the worst trip you ever took? Why was it so bad?
c. Who is your favorite relative? Why?

Share your ideas with the rest of the class.

Topic: **Personal qualities**
Language: **Asking hypothetical questions**
Focus: **Second conditionals**

PRESENTATION

1. Read about this person. Then answer the questions below.

When J. Paul Getty died in 1976, he was one of the richest people in the world. He was also one of the <u>stingiest</u>. Getty rarely turned on the heat in his home, so his guests had to wear their coats inside! He also put a pay phone inside his house for his guests to use.

a. What do you think the word *stingy* means?
b. If you were one of the richest people in the world, would you be stingy?

2. *Groups*. Classify these words in the chart below.

brave	funny	honest	lazy	stingy
dishonest	generous	irritable	loyal	thoughtful
hardworking	kind	sensitive	unreliable	
exciting	smart	easygoing	serious	
boring	tactful			

Words Used to Describe People

Good Qualities	Bad Qualities
	lazy

3. *Groups*. List five well-known people. Choose words from the box to describe each person. Then tell the class about the people you chose.

<u>James Bond:</u>
brave, exciting

<u>Mother Teresa:</u>
kind, generous

PRACTICE

1. Read questions *a–c* below. Then answer the questions at the bottom of the box.

NOTICE:
After *if*, we often use *were* instead of *was*.
  If *I were* rich, I'd …
  If *he were* a millionaire, he'd …

2. We asked someone the questions below. Match our questions with his answers.

Questions
a. If you were really rich, would you be stingy with your money?
b. If you won a large amount of money, what would you buy first?
c. If you found a wallet on the street, what would you do with it?
d. If you could change one thing about yourself, what would it be?
e. What would you do if someone were rude to you?

Answers
____ I wouldn't do anything.
____ I'd be more patient.
____ I hope not.
____ A new car for my parents.
____ I'd look for the owner's name and return it.

Listen and check your ideas. What words would you use to describe this person?

3. *Pairs.* Complete these hypothetical questions with the correct form of the verb in parentheses.

a. What would you do if you _____ someone stealing from a store? *(see)*

b. What would you do if a salesclerk _____ you too much change? *(give)*

c. What would you do if you _____ home and _____ a burglar in your house? *(come/find)*

d. What would you do if you _____ perfect English? *(speak)*

e. If you _____ the leader of your country, what would you change? *(be)*

f. If you could _____ someone else for a day, who would you like to be? *(be)*

g. If you could _____ someone famous, who would it be? *(meet)*

Take turns asking and answering the questions.

PRONUNCIATION POINT: *Sentence stress*

If you were a millionaire, what would you do with your money?

Go to page 92.

LISTENING

Paul

Marta

1. We asked two university students the questions below. Listen and write *P* next to Paul's answers and *M* next to Marta's answers.

Questions	Answers	
a. If your house were on fire and you could save only one thing, what would it be?	**P** my photographs ___ a suitcase of clothes	___ my computer ___ my stereo system
b. If you could change one thing about the world today, what would it be?	___ I'd stop all wars. ___ I'd get rid of all cars. ___ I'd destroy all guns.	___ I'd make the air cleaner. ___ I'd end hunger. ___ I'd redistribute the world's wealth.
c. If someone gave you $500, what would you do with it?	___ I'd put it in the bank. ___ I'd take my friends somewhere.	___ I'd buy a new stereo. ___ I'd buy some new clothes. ___ I'd give it to my parents.

2. *Groups.* Ask each other the questions. Then answer with your own ideas.

INTERVIEW

1. Interview three classmates and record their answers.

SURVEY QUESTIONS	PERSON 1	PERSON 2	PERSON 3
1. What would you do if you found a diamond ring on the sidewalk?			
2. What would you do if you won a million dollars?			
3. What would you do if you found a snake under your pillow?			
4. What would you do if new neighbors moved in next door to you?			
5. What would you do if you saw someone choking in a restaurant?			

When you finish, go to page 82.

PREVIEW

1. *Pairs.* Take turns asking and answering the questions below. Begin with the question in the center.

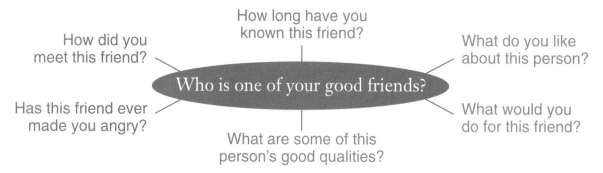

How long have you known this friend?

How did you meet this friend?

What do you like about this person?

Who is one of your good friends?

Has this friend ever made you angry?

What would you do for this friend?

What are some of this person's good qualities?

2. Get together with a new partner and tell him or her about your first partner's friend.

3. *Groups.* What are the qualities of a friend? Classify the ideas below.

be honest	have a good sense of humor
be loyal	like the same things we like
be attractive	be able to keep a secret
be creative	be a good listener
live nearby	be a hard worker
be tactful	be popular
be smart	

We *think* it's important for a friend to...	We *don't think* it's important for a friend to...
be honest	

Compare charts with another group and add three more ideas.

Example:
We think it's important for a friend to ...

READ AND RESPOND

1. What does the writer of this song promise to do for a friend? Share ideas with your classmates.

You've Got a Friend
by Carole King

When you're down[1] and troubled[2] and you need some
    loving care
And nothing, nothing is going right
Close your eyes and think of me and soon I will be there
To brighten up[3] even your darkest night.

(Refrain)
You just call out my name and you know wherever I am
I'll come running to see you again.
Winter, spring, summer, or fall,
All you have to do is call
And I'll be there: You've got a friend.

If the sky above you grows dark and full of clouds
And that old north wind begins to blow
Keep your head together[4] and call my name out loud
Soon you'll hear me knocking at your door

(Refrain)

Ain't it[5] good to know that you've got a friend
When people can be so cold[6]
They'll hurt you and desert you[7]
And take your soul if you let them
Oh but don't you let them.

(Refrain)

[1] down: sad, unhappy
[2] troubled: upset
[3] brighten (something) up: make something more cheerful or hopeful
[4] Keep your head together: stay calm
[5] Ain't it: isn't it (nonstandard English)
[6] cold: unfriendly
[7] desert you: leave you

2. *Groups.* Work together to answer these questions. Then report your group's answers to the class.

a. What are some ways that people can be "cold?"
b. What are some ways that you can "brighten up" someone's day?
c. Do you think the writer of this song is a good friend? Why or why not?

WHAT WOULD YOU DO?

1. We asked two people what they would do for a friend.
   Listen and write their answers.

What Would You Do for a Friend?

	Marie	Derrick
a. If a friend of mine were feeling down, I'd ...	*buy her flowers or a funny card.*	
b. If a friend of mine were in the hospital, I'd ...		
c. If a friend of mine were having trouble making a hard decision, I'd ...		

2. *Pairs.* What would <u>you</u> do for a friend in the same situations?
   Think of two more situations in which you would help a
   friend. Then tell what you would do to help.

   • If a friend of mine were _____
   • If a friend of mine were _____

3. *Pairs.* Read each problem situation below and tell
   what you would do. Then get together with another
   pair and share ideas.

Problem Situation	What would you do?
a. Your favorite musicians are playing tonight and you have paid a lot of money for tickets. Right before the concert, your friend calls to say she needs your help.	*We would first try to find out why she needed help. If it were for something important—if she really needed our help—we wouldn't go to the concert.*
b. Your friend asks you how you like her new hairstyle. She's very excited about it, but you think it looks horrible!	
c. A good friend suddenly stops talking to you and you don't know why.	
d. You borrow your friend's favorite jacket. You wear it to a party and then lose it.	

4. *Pairs.* Think of another problem situation and write
   it on a piece of paper. Then exchange papers with
   another pair and tell what you would do to solve
   their problem.

Topic: **Wishes**
Language: **Stating a wish**
Focus: **Wish + past tense**

PRESENTATION

1. What are the missing words in this cartoon?
   Share ideas with your classmates.

⬚ Listen and check your ideas.

2. How would you answer this question?

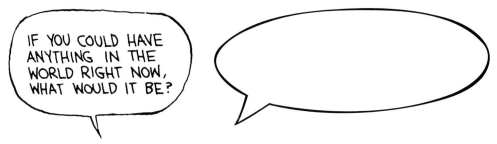

Read your answer to the class.

PRACTICE

1. Read statements *a–f* below and check (✓) *Yes* or *No*.

STATING A WISH: Wish + *past tense*	Yes	No
a. I wish I **were** taller.	❑	❑
b. I wish I **lived** alone.	❑	❑
c. I wish I **didn't have to** go to school.	❑	❑
d. I wish it **were** easier to learn a new language.	❑	❑
e. I wish I **had** more free time.	❑	❑
f. I wish I **could sing** better.	❑	❑

NOTICE:
I wish I **were** …
He wishes he **were** …

- All of the sentences above express a wish for something unlikely or impossible. What is similar about the form of the **bold-faced** verbs in these sentences?

Answer on page 103

2. Complete these wishes with the correct form of the verb in parentheses.

a. I wish I ___*knew*___ how to play the bagpipes. *(know)*
b. I wish I _____ fluent in English. *(be)*
c. I wish I _____ take a trip around the world. *(can)*
d. I wish I _____ a million dollars. *(have)*
e. I wish I _____ get up early every day. *(not/have to)*
f. I wish I _____ in a big house. *(live)*
g. I wish everyone in the world _____ the same language. *(speak)*

Compare sentences with your classmates.

🔊 PRONUNCIATION POINT: *Linked sounds*

I wish I were taller.
Go to page 92.

3. Complete the conversations below.

Ⓐ I wish it _____.
Ⓑ Why is that?
Ⓐ Because I want to go to the beach.

Ⓐ I wish I _____ every day.
Ⓑ Oh? What would you do instead?
Ⓐ I'd spend more time with my family.

Practice the conversations with a classmate.

LISTENING

📼 1. Listen and complete the conversation below. Then complete the chart.

   Ⓐ I wish I didn't have to _____.
   Ⓑ Why is that?
   Ⓐ Because I'm tired of _____.
   Ⓑ What would you do if you didn't have to _____?
   Ⓐ I'd probably _____ and earn some money.
   Ⓑ What kind of job?
   Ⓐ Oh, something interesting like working in a travel agency.

Person's Wish:	that she didn't have to ....
Details:	she's tired of ....
	would get a ....
	would like to work in a travel agency

📼 2. Listen to these conversations and take notes in the charts. Then compare charts.

a.

Person's Wish:	
Details:	

b.

Person's Wish:	
Details:	

SHARE INFORMATION

1. Write three of your own wishes.

   I wish _____.
   I wish _____.
   I wish _____.

2. *Pairs.* Listen to one of your partner's wishes and ask questions to complete the chart below.

Your Partner's Wish:	
Details:	

3. Tell the class about your partner's wish.

PREVIEW

1. *Pairs.* The pictures below illustrate the story on page 71. Match these descriptions with the pictures.

    _3_ a. The man looks very angry.
    ___ b. A sausage is stuck to the woman's nose.
    ___ c. The woman looks very unhappy.
    ___ d. There's some bread, potatoes, and a sausage on the table.
    ___ e. The woman is preparing dinner.
    ___ f. The woman looks very happy.

I wish _____
_____

I wish _____
_____

2. *Pairs.* What do you think the woman and man wished for? Complete the two wishes above.

READER'S THEATER

1. What did the man and woman wish for? Read the story and check your ideas from page 70.

THE THREE WISHES
(Part 1)

Narrator 1: There was once an old woman who lived with her husband in a small house in the country.

Narrator 2: One day, the old woman was working in her garden when she saw a cat chasing a frog. As fast as she could, the woman ran after the cat and chased it up a tree.

Frog: You saved my life, dear woman, and in return you can have three wishes.

Narrator 1: And with that the frog disappeared.

Old Woman: Three wishes? How very strange!

Narrator 2: The old woman continued working in her garden for several hours, and then she went into the house to prepare dinner for her husband.

Old Woman: Every day we have the same food for dinner. I wish I had something special to eat—something like a great big sausage!

Narrator 1: As soon as the old woman made her wish, a huge sausage appeared on the table.

Old Woman: Why look at that! I can't believe it. I wished for a sausage and there it is. And it looks so delicious!

Narrator 2: Just then, the old woman's husband arrived home.

Old Woman: Husband, husband! Our troubles are over. I saved a frog and it said I could have three wishes. And it's true because I wished for this sausage and it was suddenly here.

Old Man: What do you mean, you silly old woman? We can have three wishes and you wished for a sausage! How stupid you are! I wish that sausage were stuck to your nose.

Narrator 1: All at once the woman gave a cry, for the sausage was stuck to her nose. She pulled and pulled at it, but she couldn't get it off.

To be continued ...

2. *Groups.* Listen to the recorded version of the story. Then assign roles and read the story aloud.

FINISH THE STORY

1. *Groups.* How do you want the story to end?
   Work together to answer these questions.

   a. What does the old woman say when she can't get the sausage off her nose?
   b. What does the old man say to his wife?
   c. How do the old man and old woman use their third wish?
   d. How do they feel at the end of the story? What do they say to each other?

2. *Groups.* Use your answers to the questions in Activity 1 to write an ending to "The Three Wishes."

3. *Groups.* Practice and perform your story for your classmates.

> <u>Narrator 1</u>: All at once the woman gave a cry, for the sausage was stuck to her nose. She pulled and pulled at it, but she couldn't get it off.
>
> <u>Old Woman</u>: Help! Husband, the sausage is stuck to my nose!
>
> <u>Old Man</u>:

4. Listen to this version of the end of the story. Is it the same as yours?

BE CAREFUL WHAT YOU WISH FOR

1. *Groups.* Work together to think of three wishes. Write them on the lines below.

   Example:
   We wish everyone in the world spoke the same language.

   _____
   _____
   _____

   List your group's wishes on the board.

2. *Groups.* Choose one of the wishes. What would happen if this wish came true? List two good things and two bad things. Then present your group's ideas to the class.

   Example:
   We wish everyone in the world spoke the same language.

   Good Things
   If everyone in the world spoke the same language …
   … I wouldn't have to learn English.
   … it would be much easier to travel in foreign countries.

   Bad Things
   If everyone in the world spoke the same language …
   … language teachers would all lose their jobs.
   … the world would be less interesting.

Topic: **Feelings**
Language: **Describing feelings**
Focus: **Participles as adjectives**

PRESENTATION

1. *Pairs.* What are these people thinking? Write your ideas.

a.   b.   c.

2. How would you feel in these situations? Answer the questions.
Then compare answers with your classmates.

a. How would you feel if you were the only
person who dressed up for a party?

b. How would you feel if you invited some
friends to dinner and no one showed up?

c. How would you feel if you were chosen
from the audience to come up on stage?

proud	uncomfortable
embarrassed	nervous
confused	surprised
happy	angry
irritated	excited
disappointed	sad

3. *Pairs.* Think of three ways to complete
this question.

How would you feel if …?

Ask your classmates your questions.

PRACTICE

1. Read sentences *a–f* below and check (✓) *True* or *False*.

> **DESCRIBING FEELINGS:** *Participles as adjectives*
>
> | | True | False |
> |---|---|---|
> | a. Sometimes I feel **bored**. | ❏ | ❏ |
> | b. I feel pretty **relaxed** right now. | ❏ | ❏ |
> | c. I would be **terrified** if I had to give a speech. | ❏ | ❏ |
> | d. I think it would be **boring** to watch TV all day. | ❏ | ❏ |
> | e. I think a hot bath is **relaxing**. | ❏ | ❏ |
> | f. Earthquakes are **terrifying**. | ❏ | ❏ |
>
> • Which sentences describe how someone feels?
> • When do we use adjectives that end in *-ed*?
> • When do we use adjectives that end in *-ing*?
>
> **Answers on page 104**

2. Complete these sentences. Tell what you think.
   Then compare ideas with your classmates.

   a. When I'm tired, I like to _____.
   b. I feel relaxed when I _____.
   c. I would be frightened if I _____.

   d. I think it's tiring to _____.
   e. I think it's relaxing to _____.
   f. I think it's frightening to _____.

3. Choose a word to complete each sentence. Then
   compare ideas with a partner.

   a. Ⓐ Did you hear the news? Ken and Tina are getting married!
      Ⓑ Really! That's _____! I thought they hated each
        other! (*amazed/amazing*)

   b. Ⓐ I'm so _____. I failed my driving test again.
        (*discouraged/discouraging*)
      Ⓑ Don't worry. You'll do better next time.

   c. Ⓐ Your trip sounds really _____! (*excited/exciting*)
      Ⓑ Thanks. I'm really looking forward to it.

   d. Ⓐ Could you repeat what you just said? I'm _____.
        (*confused/confusing*)
      Ⓑ Sure. No problem.

   e. Ⓐ How was the concert?
      Ⓑ Long and _____. I fell asleep! (*bored/boring*)

   f. Ⓐ Did you remember to send your sister a birthday card?
      Ⓑ No, I forgot! I'm so _____! (*embarrassed/embarrassing*)

▭ **Listen and check your answers.**

▭ PRONUNCIATION POINT: *Syllable stress*

● •   ◎   • ●
angry   amazed

Go to page 92.

LISTENING

**1. Choose a word to complete each conversation.
Then share ideas with your classmates.**

> bored   annoyed   tired   excited

a.   **A** You look _____.
    B I am. Mario was supposed to call and he didn't.

b.   **A** What are you so _____ about?
    B I got the job I wanted! I can't believe it.
    A That's great! When do you start?
    B In two weeks.

c.   **A** You look _____.
    B I am. I've been waiting for an hour.
    A Don't you have anything to read?
    B No. I forgot to bring something.

d.   **A** How about another set?
    B No, thanks. I'm really _____.
    A Oh, come on. We just started.
    B What do you mean? We've been playing for two hours.

**Listen and check your ideas. Then practice the
conversations with a partner.**

**2. Listen to these conversations and take notes in
the chart below.**

The person feels ...	Because ...
1. *excited*	*he's going to France*
2.	
3.	
4.	
5.	

**3. *Pairs*. Write your own conversation. Then role-play
the situation for your classmates. Below are some
ways you could start your conversation.**

What's the matter?   Are you okay?   You look ____.
Is something wrong?   Do you feel okay?

PREVIEW

1. *Groups.* These pictures show memorable moments in two
   people's lives. Study the pictures below and answer the questions.

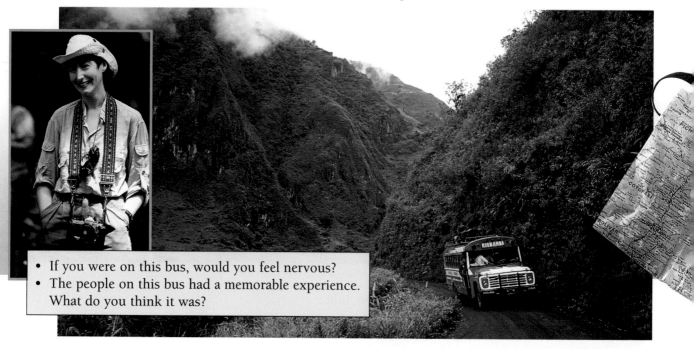

- If you were on this bus, would you feel nervous?
- The people on this bus had a memorable experience.
  What do you think it was?

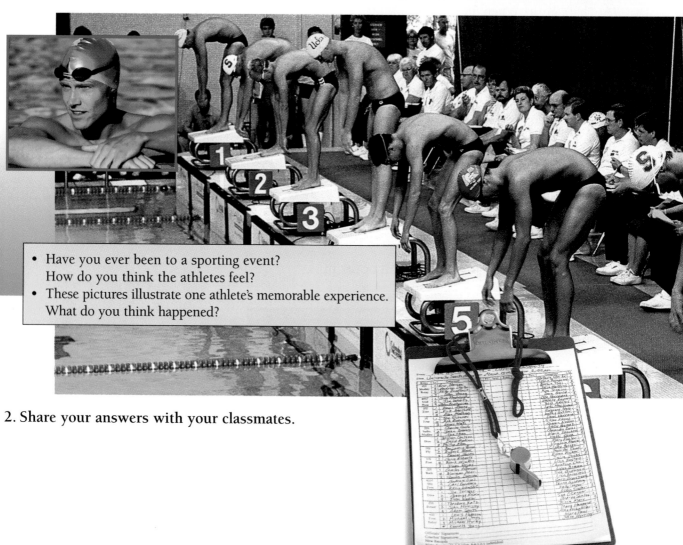

- Have you ever been to a sporting event?
  How do you think the athletes feel?
- These pictures illustrate one athlete's memorable experience.
  What do you think happened?

2. Share your answers with your classmates.

READ AND ASK QUESTIONS

1. Choose a word to complete each story below. Then compare ideas with your classmates.

amazed	excited	embarrassed	terrified
amazing	exciting	embarrassing	terrifying

MEMORABLE MOMENTS

a.

"Several years ago, I took a bus trip in the mountains. It was an old bus and it was full of people. I was sitting in the second row, just behind the driver. At one point, the bus driver stopped the bus on the mountain road. He got out to look at something but he forgot to put on the brake. Suddenly, the bus began to move! It started rolling away from the driver toward the edge of the mountain. I was _____! ..."

b.

"A friend of mine had a pretty _____ experience. He was a very fast swimmer and he raced on his university swim team. One day the swim team was at a big competition. My friend was pretty nervous and he forgot to do something important—he forgot to tie his swimsuit! So when he dove into the water, his swimsuit started to come off! ..."

2. *Pairs.* Together think of a question you'd like to ask the speaker of each story.

Questions	Answers
a.	
b.	

3. Listen to the complete stories to find answers to your questions. Share any answers you find.

INTERVIEW

1. List some memorable moments in your life.

Example:
the time I got lost in New York
the time I met _____
the time I went skydiving
my brother's wedding
my first date

2. Choose a memorable moment that you feel
comfortable talking about. Then complete
this sentence.

_____ was a memorable moment for me.

3. *Pairs.* Interview each other about your memorable
moments. Ask questions to get the important details.
Take notes on your partner's answers.

Why...?   How...?

Who...? ——(Questions)—— When...?

What...?   Where...?

4. Tell the class about your partner's memorable moment.

ASK AND ANSWER

3. Look at Team B's questions about this painting. Then read the information below and answer their questions. Write each question and answer on a separate piece of paper. If you don't know the answer, write: *We don't know*.

Example:
Who is the man?
He is the young woman's father.

Blessing on the Wedding Day
   "This is a cousin's wedding. The bridesmaid is waiting to put the veil on the bride, the father is waiting at the doorway, the grandmother is all dressed and ready to go. Then all of a sudden, everyone gets very quiet because the mother of the bride says it's time for her to bless her daughter. She asks the daughter to kneel down on a cushion.
   "The daughter is about to leave her parents' house. This is the mother's opportunity to bless her daughter, give her advice, and send her off on the next phase of her life. It's a very special moment."
—Carmen Lomas Garza

4. Give Team B its list of questions and your answers. Invite them to look at the picture on page 6 while they read the questions and answers.

ASK AND ANSWER

3. Look at Team A's questions about this painting. Then read the information below and answer their questions. Write each question and answer on a separate piece of paper. If you don't know the answer, write: *We don't know.*

Example:
Where are these people?
They are at Aunt Paz and
    Uncle Beto's house.

Empanadas

"Once every year, my Aunt Paz and Uncle Beto would make dozens and dozens of empanadas, sweet turnovers filled with sweet potato or squash from their garden. They would invite all the relatives and friends to come over, and you could eat as many as you wanted. They lived in a little one-bedroom house, and every surface in the house was covered with a plate of empanadas. There was no place to sit down.

"There's Uncle Beto, rolling out the dough. Aunt Paz, in the yellow dress with the red flowers, is spreading in the filling. My mother and father are drinking coffee. That's me in the blue dress."
—Carmen Lomas Garza

sweet potato

squash

4. Give Team A its list of questions and your answers. Invite them to look at the picture on page 6 while they read the questions and answers.

Unit 2 PERSON A

SHARE INFORMATION

Study the signs below for one minute.
Then go back to page 9.

This sign means "stop."

This sign means "end of highway." It tells drivers to slow down.

This sign means "pedestrian area." Cars are not allowed here.

Unit 11

THE THREE WISHES (Part 2)

... continued from page 71

Old Woman:	Help! Husband, the sausage is stuck to my nose.
Old Man:	Just calm down, calm down. Don't worry. I'll get it off.
Narrator 2:	The old man grabbed the sausage and pulled with all his strength. He pulled and he pulled, but he couldn't get it off his wife's nose.
Old Woman:	(Crying) Oh no, what are we going to do? We only have one wish left and I have this stupid sausage on my nose! Oh, how unlucky I am! (she cries)
Old Man:	Okay, okay. Stop crying and I'll make the last wish. (sighs) I wish ... I wish that the sausage were on the table instead of on my wife's nose.
Narrator 1:	Immediately the sausage fell off the old woman's nose and landed on the table. The old woman gave a cry of joy.
Old Woman:	Oh, husband! Thank goodness! It's off! Oh, how lucky I am!
Narrator 2:	The old man and the old woman were so happy that they jumped up and down and danced around the house. And that's the end of the story.

Unit 2 TEAM B

SHARE INFORMATION

Study the signs below for one minute.
Then go back to page 9.

This sign means "don't feed the baboons."

This sign means "beware of camels." It tells drivers to be careful because camels like to cross the road here.

The top symbol on this sign means means "beware of crocodiles." The bottom symbol means "no swimming."

Unit 10

INTERVIEW

2. What were the survey questions on page 63 really asking? Match the questions.

Survey Questions
- ❏ 1. What would you do if you found a diamond ring on the sidewalk?
- ❏ 2. What would you do if you won a million dollars?
- ❏ 3. What would you do if you found a snake under your pillow?
- ❏ 4. What would you do if new neighbors moved in next door to you?
- ❏ 5. What would you do if you saw someone choking in a restaurant?

a. How brave are you?
b. How quick-thinking are you?
c. How generous are you?
d. How honest are you?
e. How friendly are you?

3. *Groups.* Look back at the answers to the survey questions on page 63. What do they tell you about your classmates?

READ AND SHARE INFORMATION

3. Read the information below and look for answers to your questions about Nicholas Alkemade from page 25.

THE BURNING AIRPLANE

During World War II, Nicholas Alkemade was a sergeant in the British Royal Air Force. On March 25, 1944, he was flying on a mission when his airplane caught on fire. As the fire spread, the pilot and the other crew members quickly put on their parachutes and jumped out of the burning plane. However, the fire destroyed Alkemade's parachute before he could reach it. Nicholas Alkemade had to make a decision—should he burn in the airplane or jump without a parachute?

Alkemade decided to jump. When Alkemade jumped, his plane was flying 6,000 meters above ground. He fell quickly, moving at about 185 km/h. But he didn't die.

Alkemade was very lucky. He survived because he landed in a forest of fir trees. The thick branches slowed his fall and the ground he landed on was covered in about 45 cm of soft snow.

Amazingly, Alkemade was not seriously injured. He had burns on his legs, hands, and face from the fire. His back and his right knee were hurt, and he had a cut on his head. But he didn't break any bones. Nicholas Alkemade survived the war and lived to be an old man.

4. Answer your partner's questions about Nicholas Alkemade.

5. Look back at page 25. Ask your partner your questions about Ann Hodges.

READ AND SHARE INFORMATION

3. Read the information below and look for answers to your
   questions about Ann Hodges from page 25.

The Big Bang

Ann Hodges was a housewife in Sylacauga, Alabama, in the United States.
On the afternoon of November 30, 1954, something very unusual happened to her.
On that day, Mrs. Hodges was not feeling well and was taking a nap on the sofa in
her living room. Suddenly, she was awakened by a loud bang and a sharp pain in her
left hip. She looked around and noticed that there was a hole in her ceiling and that
some of her furniture was broken.

On the floor next to Mrs. Hodges was a grapefruit-sized rock. It was a meteorite—a
piece of rock from outer space! It was black and weighed about 5 kg. The meteorite was
traveling at over 300 km/h when it crashed through Mrs. Hodges' roof. It passed through her
living room ceiling, bounced off a piece of furniture, then hit Mrs. Hodges on the hip.

Incredibly, Mrs. Hodges was not seriously injured. She only had bruises on her hip
and hand. Mrs. Hodges died in 1972 and remains the only person in history ever to be
injured by a meteorite. The meteorite is currently in a museum at the University of Alabama.

4. Look back at page 25. Ask your partner your
   questions about Nicholas Alkemade.

5. Answer your partner's questions about
   Ann Hodges.

SHARE INFORMATION

2. Person B: Use your chart to answer your partner's questions. Then ask your partner questions to complete the chart below.

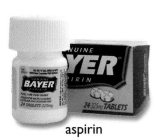
aspirin

fireworks

ink   the zipper

Example:
A Do you know when aspirin was invented?
B Yes. It was invented in 1853.

Invention	Where?	When?	Description
Aspirin		1853	It was made from the bark (the outside part) of a _____.
Fireworks	China		They were used to scare away evil spirits.
Ink	China and Egypt		The first ink was made of soot, water, and plant material.
The zipper		1893	The first zipper was used on a pair of _____.

3. *Pairs. Use your charts to answer these questions.*

   a. Which invention is the oldest?
   b. Which invention do you think is the most useful? Why?

PREVIEW

3. Match each picture with a description below.
   Write the letter of the picture.

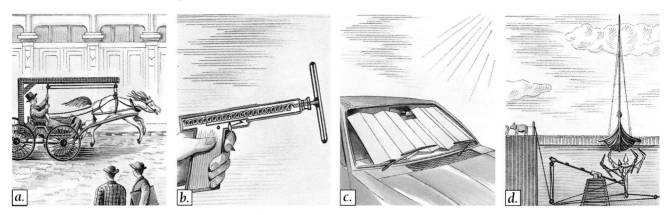

❑ This giant claw was invented by the Greek mathematician and engineer Archimedes (287–212 B.C.). It was designed to hide under the water in a harbor. If an enemy ship entered the harbor, the claw could grab the ship, lift it up, and shake it until the people fell out.

❑ In the 19th century, city streets were filled with people walking and horses pulling carriages. A big problem was runaway horses. If a horse got frightened, it could cause a serious accident. A simple solution to the problem was proposed by the inventor of this device. By pulling on a rope, the driver could pull the frightened horse up off the ground and avoid an accident.

❑ This device was invented to solve the problem of flies. When the trigger was pulled, a coiled spring released the flat rubber head into the air or against a wall.

❑ When a car sits in the hot sun, it gets really hot inside. This device was invented to prevent that from happening. All you have to do is unfold it and put it in the windshield to block the sun.

4. *Pairs.* Work together to answer these questions.

   a. Which device do you think is the oldest? Why?
   b. Only one of these items was ever used. Which one is it?
   c. Why do you think the other three devices weren't ever used?

Unit 12

MEMORABLE MOMENTS

a.

"Several years ago, I took a bus trip in the mountains. It was an old bus and it was full of people. I was sitting in the second row, just behind the driver. At one point, the bus driver stopped the bus on the mountain road. He got out to look at something but he forgot to put on the brake. Suddenly, the bus began to move! It started rolling away from the driver toward the edge of the mountain. I was terrified!

"Without thinking, I ran forward and jumped into the driver's seat and quickly stepped on the brake. When the bus stopped, everyone in the bus cheered. I was the hero of the day."

b.

"A friend of mine had a pretty embarrassing experience. He was a very fast swimmer and he raced on his university swim team. One day the swim team was at a big competition. My friend was pretty nervous and he forgot to do something important—he forgot to tie his swimsuit! So when he dove into the water, his swimsuit started to come off!

"My friend didn't want to lose the race, so he didn't stop. He kept on swimming and before long, his swimsuit came off altogether. Everyone was laughing, but my friend didn't stop. He just kept on swimming. As soon as the race was over he quickly swam over to his swimsuit and put it back on. Everyone was laughing and cheering. Even though he didn't win the race that day I think everyone admired him for still finishing."

ARCTI

ICELAND

NORWAY
SWEDEN
FINLAND

ESTONIA
LATVIA
DENMARK
LITHUANIA
UNITED
KINGDOM
IRELAND
BELARUS
POLAND
EUROPE
NET
BEL
GERMANY
CZE
SLOVAKIA
UKRAINE
FRANCE
SWI
LIE
AUS
HUNGARY
MOL
SLO
CRO
ROMANIA
AND
BOS
ITALY
YUG
BULGARIA
SPAIN
MAC
GEORGIA
PORTUGAL
VC
GREECE
TURKEY
ARM
AZE

RUSSIA

ASIA

KAZAKHSTAN

MONGOLIA

UZBEKISTAN
KYRGYZSTAN
TURKMENISTAN
TAJIKISTAN

N. KOREA
S. KOREA
JAPAN

CYP
SYRIA
LEB
ISR
IRAQ
IRAN
JORDAN
AFGHANISTAN
CHINA
TAIWAN

MOROCCO
TUNISIA
KUW
QAT
UAE
PAKISTAN
NEPAL
BHUTAN

WESTERN
SAHARA
ALGERIA
LIBYA
EGYPT
SAUDI
ARABIA
OMAN
INDIA
BURMA
(MYANMAR)
LAOS

AFRICA

MAURITANIA
MALI
NIGER
CHAD
ERI
YEMEN
BANGLADESH
THAILAND
VIETNAM
PHILIPPINES

SEN
GAM
BURKINA
FASO
SUDAN
DJI
CAMBODIA

GUB
GUINEA
GHANA
NIGERIA
SRI
LANKA
MALAYSIA

SIERRA
LEONE
TOGO
BENIN
CAR
ETHIOPIA
SINGAPORE
BORNEO

LIBERIA
COTE
D'IVOIRE
EQG
CAMEROON
UGANDA
KENYA
SOMALIA

PAPUA
NEW GUINEA

GABON
CONGO
ZAIRE
RWA
BUR
TANZANIA
INDONESIA

INDIAN OCEAN
Bali

ANGOLA
ZAMBIA
MALAWI
MADAGASCAR

NAMIBIA
ZIMBABWE
MOZAMBIQUE

BOTSWANA
SWAZILAND

AUSTRALIA

SOUTH
AFRICA
LESOTHO

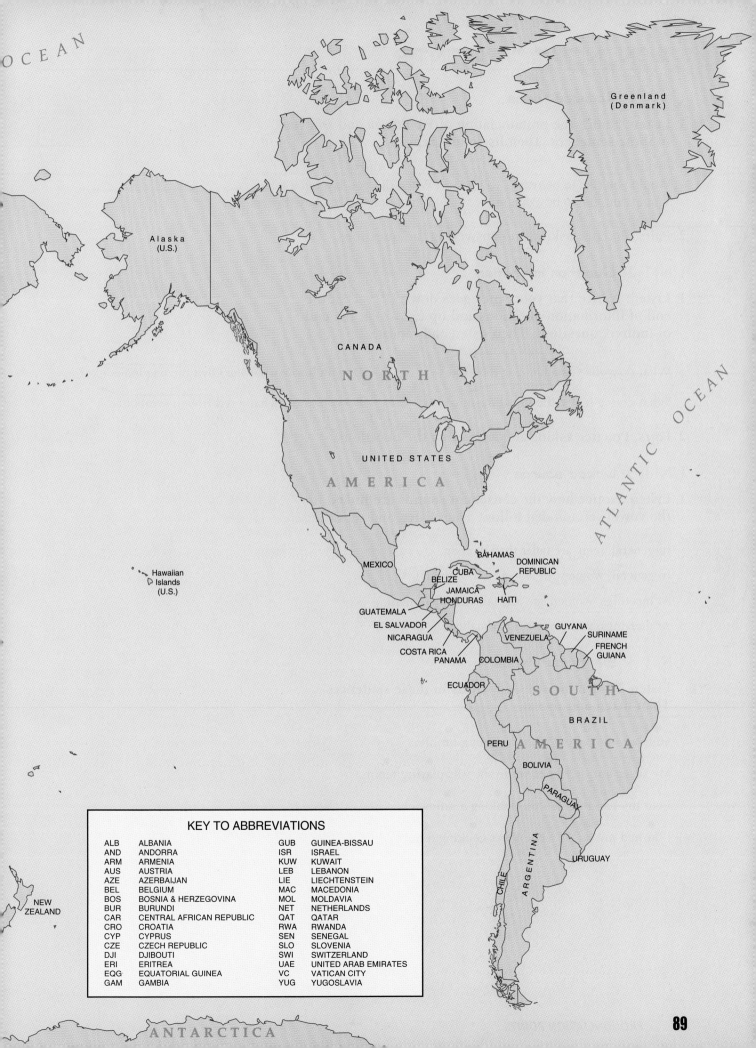

OCEAN

Greenland
(Denmark)

Alaska
(U.S.)

CANADA

N O R T H

ATLANTIC OCEAN

UNITED STATES

A M E R I C A

Hawaiian
Islands
(U.S.)

MEXICO

BAHAMAS
DOMINICAN
CUBA   REPUBLIC
BELIZE
JAMAICA
HONDURAS   HAITI
GUATEMALA
EL SALVADOR
NICARAGUA   VENEZUELA
COSTA RICA
PANAMA   COLOMBIA

GUYANA
SURINAME
FRENCH
GUIANA

ECUADOR

S O U T H

BRAZIL

PERU   A M E R I C A

BOLIVIA

PARAGUAY

CHILE

ARGENTINA

URUGUAY

NEW
ZEALAND

KEY TO ABBREVIATIONS

ALB	ALBANIA	GUB	GUINEA-BISSAU
AND	ANDORRA	ISR	ISRAEL
ARM	ARMENIA	KUW	KUWAIT
AUS	AUSTRIA	LEB	LEBANON
AZE	AZERBAIJAN	LIE	LIECHTENSTEIN
BEL	BELGIUM	MAC	MACEDONIA
BOS	BOSNIA & HERZEGOVINA	MOL	MOLDAVIA
BUR	BURUNDI	NET	NETHERLANDS
CAR	CENTRAL AFRICAN REPUBLIC	QAT	QATAR
CRO	CROATIA	RWA	RWANDA
CYP	CYPRUS	SEN	SENEGAL
CZE	CZECH REPUBLIC	SLO	SLOVENIA
DJI	DJIBOUTI	SWI	SWITZERLAND
ERI	ERITREA	UAE	UNITED ARAB EMIRATES
EQG	EQUATORIAL GUINEA	VC	VATICAN CITY
GAM	GAMBIA	YUG	YUGOSLAVIA

A N T A R C T I C A

PRONUNCIATION POINTS

UNIT 1: Reduced forms

1. Listen. Notice the pronunciation of *Would you* and *Did you* in these sentences. Then listen and repeat.

/wʊdʒə/
Would you like to be rich?
Would you like to be a doctor?

/dɪdʒə/
When did you last tell a joke?
When did you last buy flowers?

2. *Pairs*. Practice asking and answering the questions.

UNIT 2: Question intonation

1. Listen. Notice that your voice goes down (⟍) at the end of information questions and up (⟋) at the end of indirect questions. Then listen and repeat.

What does the Canadian flag look like?

Do you know what the Olympic flag looks like?

What does a red traffic signal mean?

Do you know what a red ribbon symbolizes?

2. *Pairs*. Practice asking and answering the questions.

UNIT 3: Linked sounds

1. Listen. Notice how the consonant sounds are linked to the vowel sounds that follow. Then listen and repeat.

In general, men are taller than women.

In general, women are not as tall as men.

At meetings, women are less talkative than men.

At meetings, women are not as talkative as men.

UNIT 4: Sentence stress

Listen. Notice the stressed words in these sentences. Then listen and repeat.

Sullivan was fishing when lightning hit him.

My sister hurt her knee while she was playing tennis.

I cut my hand while I was making a sandwich.

I burned my finger while I was cooking dinner.